Advance praise for *Your Lovable Lawyer's Guide to Legal Wellness*

"Danny Karon capably delivers as promised in his new book *Your Lovable Lawyer's Guide to Legal Wellness.* They say laughter is the best medicine, and he uses humor to ease the challenge of conveying practical legal information that will help people through many common and serious situations to the benefit of themselves and their families. Easy and informative, *Your Lovable Lawyer's Guide to Legal Wellness* is a highly worthwhile read!"

—Richard A. Cordray, former director of the Consumer Financial Protection Bureau of the United States

"In *Your Loveable Lawyer's Guide to Legal Wellness*, Danny Karon has drawn on his extensive experience as a successful lawyer and dedicated advocate to create a comprehensive resource that provides invaluable information for anyone navigating real-life, day-to-day legal challenges. He has the unique knack for presenting information in an understandable and entertaining way that will capture your attention and stay with you long after you finish reading his wonderful book."

—Stuart T. Rossman, former director of litigation for the National Consumer Law Center

"Danny Karon believes you are getting legally screwed, and he is likely right. His new book offers legal first aid with the goal of helping you achieve a state of "legal wellness." His book is such great fun to read that he belongs on late-night TV alongside Stephen Colbert and Jimmy Fallon. Read it and see!"

—Professor John C. Coffee, Jr., Adolf A. Berle Professor of Law and director of the Center on Corporate Governance at Columbia Law School

"Danny Karon is the Suze Orman of the law—a popular, accessible, and respected sage for every man, woman, and child. But there is one difference: He is also entertaining as hell. Not only will you be unable to put this book down, but you will also want to read it again and again, then share it with your family and friends."

—Professor Brian T. Fitzpatrick, Milton R. Underwood Chair in Free Enterprise and professor of law at Vanderbilt Law School

"Lawyers are people, too. Who knew? Danny Karon proves this point in *Your Lovable Lawyer's Guide to Legal Wellness,* where he provides us with tools to become better problem solvers and better people, to boot—all with an extra helping of fun in the process."

—Elizabeth J. Cabraser, Lieff Cabraser Heimann & Bernstein, LLP

your lovable lawyer's guide to legal wellness

your lovable lawyer's guide to legal wellness

FIGHTING BACK Against a World That's Out to CHEAT YOU

danny karon

SAVIO REPVBLIC

A SAVIO REPUBLIC BOOK
An Imprint of Post Hill Press
ISBN: 979-8-89565-083-7
ISBN (eBook): 979-8-89565-084-4

Your Lovable Lawyer's Guide to Legal Wellness:
Fighting Back Against a World That's Out to Cheat You

Cover Design by Cody Corcoran

This book, as well as any other Savio Republic publications, may be purchased in bulk quantities at a special discounted rate. Contact orders@posthillpress.com for more information.

All people, locations, events, and situations are portrayed to the best of the author's memory. While all of the events described are true, many names and identifying details have been changed to protect the privacy of the people involved.

A portion of the author's proceeds will be donated to the Legal Aid Society of Cleveland.

This book is intended for informational purposes only and does not constitute legal, accounting, tax, financial, or other professional or nonprofessional advice. Reading this book or any communication with the author does not create an attorney-client relationship. No attorney-client privilege or confidentiality is established by reading this book or contacting the author regarding its contents. Laws vary by jurisdiction and change continually, and the book's content may not reflect the laws applicable to any specific issue in any particular jurisdiction and may not be the most current law on any specific issue in any particular jurisdiction. Readers should consult a licensed attorney for advice regarding their particular legal issues or circumstances. The author and publisher disclaim any liability for actions taken or not taken based on the information contained in this book. By purchasing or reading this book, in whole or in part, you agree to all of the foregoing. To reject these terms, you must return the book unread. The author rejects any additional or varying terms.

posthillpress.com
New York • Nashville
Published in the United States of America

1 2 3 4 5 6 7 8 9 10

To my wife Mimi, who always believed in me; to my kids Giliann and Morgan, who always inspired me; to my mom, dad, and brother, who always supported me; and to my in-laws, who always encouraged me.

Table of Contents

Chapter 1
Legal wellness and why it's so essential

When the airline cancels your flight and won't rebook you, what can you do?

When your cell phone provider slips a secret charge into your bill yet won't credit you, what can you do?

When someone says something defamatory about you online, what can you do?

When companies big or small screw you over or when you get caught up in everyday situations that could have legal consequences, you don't have to roll over. I'm going to help you.

If you don't know how the law applies to these everyday situations, it's probably just a matter of time before you get stepped on or worse. And that's where this book comes in. Importantly, this book is not legal *advice*. Without an attorney-client relationship with you, I lack the ability to apply my knowledge to your situation, meaning I can't know how the law affects your legal rights and give you legal advice. Instead, this book is legal *information*—information that's essential to preserving or restoring your legal wellness.

Because of this, I won't tell you what to do. Instead, I'll identify and explain what's happening to you and around you, so you can suitably deal with it. My goal is to help keep you from getting into trouble, help get you out of trouble the next time you find yourself in it, or both.

Let's face it, troubles like the three examples at the start of this chapter cost you time and money. They can also take an emotional toll. After all, when you're in dire legal straits, often you're also in dire financial and emotional straits. That's because when you have a legal problem, you're spending time and money, and you're probably freaking out. But with some aptitude for the law, you can hopefully avoid troubling legal situations.

What's more, legal troubles can also affect the people around you. For instance, when an airline screws you, you complain to your partner or friends, right? Why let this happen when you can learn how to avoid legal pitfalls in the first place? Yes, it's possible—and easy—to take your legal wellness into your hands!

Knowing your rights is essential because the law affects so much of our lives at a subtextual level that's often difficult to see, realize, and understand. But when you're done reading this book, you'll feel empowered. You'll have confidence in, and an aptitude for, the law that you didn't think you could get short of going to law school. You don't need to be a lawyer to promote your legal rights.

Think of this book and its mission this way: We all have cars, but we don't know how to fix them, right? We all have bodies, but we don't know how to treat them. We all have furnaces, but we don't know how to service them. The list is endless.

As it concerns what I call your *legal self*, all of us are affected by product sellers, other drivers, medical professionals, etc. That list is endless, too. But often, we don't know how to take care of our legal selves. We don't know how to spot many of the legal issues that affect us, we don't know what rights and remedies we have, and we don't know how to resolve the legal issues that eventually plague most of us. In addition to all this, we often don't know where to turn for legal help.

But what if I told you that sometimes you needn't turn anywhere, which also means you needn't spend money on a lawyer? What if I shared a few legal guidelines for you to navigate that empowered you to identify legal pitfalls and avoid legal issues *before* they happened? That's the point of this book: to raise your legal awareness, so you either can avoid legal issues from the get-go or know how to deal with them suitably if you can't. Indeed, as far as the law goes, an ounce of prevention *is* worth a pound of cure.

For over three decades, I've worked tirelessly for consumers, recovering over $10 billion for hundreds of millions of people and small businesses. My hard work has brought me considerable media exposure. I appear frequently on Fox News, NewsNation, and Scripps News. Also, I've appeared on CNN and CBS News and in *USA Today*, *The New York Post*, *Bloomberg*, *MarketWatch*, and more. I've received several industry awards, including America's Most Honored Lawyers, National Trial Lawyers—Top 100, and America's Top 100 High Stakes Litigators, among others.

And because I've long believed teaching—meaning, paying forward what we know and have experienced—is my profession's highest calling, I've also taught law school for years.

I began by teaching complex litigation at Columbia Law School in New York City. But when the weekly commute from Cleveland became a bit more than I could manage, I knew I needed something within driving distance from home. So I began alternating between the University of Michigan Law School and The Ohio State University Moritz College of Law, where I teach consumer class actions and complex litigation. Sure, the pay is peanuts but ask any law professor who practices why they do it, and they'll tell you the same thing: It ain't the money.

How 'bout this: Instead of telling you *that* I've gone to the mat to protect your rights, I'll show you precisely *how* I have. A few years ago, enforcement officials from across the globe busted the leading manufacturers of flat-panel screens for computer monitors, TVs, and laptops. Products you own—and likely lots of them. Turned out that for over a decade, these companies were operating a global scheme to fix prices on the screens we buy and use every day.

The manufacturers' goal? To line their pockets and fleece you, of course. This was a problem that required fixing. I needed to figure out how to get buyers their money back for having overpaid for electronic devices that utilized these flat panels.

And never mind that these companies cooked up their worldwide money-making scheme in Taiwan, Korea, and Japan. I was bent on getting *American* consumers their money back from these companies. But where in the world—literally—was I going to start?

Because these cases are big and expensive and involve some of the most well-heeled defense firms in the world, I got together with some like-minded, consumer-attorney friends and, as they say, made a federal case of it. And after almost a decade of expensive and risky hard-fought litigation against these price fixers, we finally resolved the case for nearly $2 billion—money that went back into the pockets of consumers like you. Perhaps you even remember getting your check!

Now, here's some inside baseball. Despite massive amounts of evidence of the manufacturers' guilt, this case took as long as it did because they simply didn't want to own up to what they'd done. Shameless, don't you think?

I mean, you would never teach your kids to evade responsibility like that, so why was it okay for the flat-panel manufacturers to do so for almost a decade? Because, sad to say, that's how big business operates. It's how corporate America works. And without legal aptitude, you're often helpless to hold big business accountable. You may not even recognize when you've been victimized in the first place.

This is why you need to push and fight. If you believe you're right, pursue your cause. Sure, it might take some time, but keep pushing, asking questions, and standing up for yourself. That's the only way to end up on top. And when that happens, you won't mind the time and effort it took; you'll just relish your victory.

Here's the deal: I hate seeing people get screwed over. But unlike other lawyers, I speak your language. *Our* language. I couldn't teach this stuff at our country's top law schools if I didn't. As I do with my law students, I'll help you to understand what you need to know, and I'll deliver my message in plain English—not ugly legalese. After all, if I'm not delivering a supportive, sensible, and helpful message, I'm wasting your time and mine.

So if you've ever felt helpless and ignored and didn't know what to do when you got screwed over (or if you could use some help figuring out *whether* you've been screwed over), this book is for you. And even if you work *for* the man, you're still a consumer. That means, sorry to say, you, too, are susceptible to being screwed—even by your own employer.

Now, a whole lot of material follows—notably, letters I've written for myself, friends, and clients—but I certainly don't expect you to rigorously scour the chapters or commit them to memory. That would be far too much work. Instead, I intend for my legal information to provide tools for your rapidly growing legal self-help toolbox—tools you can begin using when addressing *your* unique situations.

So, for instance, let's say you have a problem with your landlord, as my son's friends did in Chapter 14. You'd go to that chapter to learn first that just because you're the tenant, you needn't take what your landlord is dishing out. Instead, leases often include language useful to you; language you can use to fight back. You'd then read my letter and extract from it those nuggets and concepts that are useful to you—tidbits that either *resemble* your situation ("Hey, my landlord is also accusing *me* of having pet when I don't!") or from which you can *extrapolate* to fit your situation ("Hey, my landlord is accusing me of having neglected my property, and Danny's letter describes how he handled the landlord's accusation of his son's friends having *destroyed* their property.").

You see, by treating my book as a living document, you'll have a catalog of information you can draw from when misfortune comes *your* way, as it routinely does mine and my clients'.

So if you're beginning to understand that all of us are at risk, you're right—just look at who the flat-panel manufacturers targeted. This means it's not a matter of whether you'll get screwed over; it's a matter of when. And while plenty of people don't do anything because they don't know they can, you don't have to fall into that category. With the proper mindset and a few tools, you can stand up and start protecting *your* legal wellness.

Chapter 2
Who is Your Lovable Lawyer?

I didn't become a lawyer for the money. Far from it. Had I wanted only to make money, I could have done plenty of other things. I became a lawyer because I wanted to make a difference. I wanted to solve problems. I wanted to help people.

The work I do for consumers is called contingent-fee work, meaning, if I don't win for my clients, I don't get paid. Talk about taking your work home with you! So when I talk about caring and doing well by folks, I'm right there with you, walking the walk.

This might beg the question, "Why would you put yourself and your family at such risk?" Most people get up, go to work, and get paid no matter what. I suppose you can blame (or thank) my dad. Like me, he's a plaintiff's lawyer, meaning he works for injured people, not big corporations. I grew up seeing people get the short end of the stick, but I also saw how it looked and felt to help them. When I heard about my dad's cases and causes, I knew I wanted to help people, too.

Considering this, I didn't want to work for the "dark side"—the companies who shamelessly count beans and calculate how many people they can afford to cheat, hurt, or kill before it's no longer profitable for their shareholders. There would be nothing satisfying or commendable about helping those clients. I knew that wouldn't make me proud, the way helping real people would. (For the record, I doubt there are any books on the market that teach legal wellness from the *corporate* perspective—complete with chapters on how to screw consumers and feel good about it.)

The way I see it, there's a reason John Grisham writes books and Hollywood produces movies about what *I* do instead of what corporate defense lawyers do. Readers want a story with high stakes. They want a hero who could lose everything fighting for something bigger than themselves. There's no grit, romance, fear, uncertainty, terror, or risk in getting paid per hour as defense lawyers do. But there's a whole lot of those things in getting paid *perhaps,* as I do.

What's more, in my thirty-four years of practice, I've observed a societal bias against access to justice where people who need it the most tend to get it the least. This means people often don't know they have a legal problem that deserves attention. Or if they do, they don't know how to solve it or how to find a lawyer to help them. This kind of discrimination and disenfranchisement is not okay.

We're living in an age where people crave wellness. Just look at Dr. Phil's audience, eager to obtain emotional wellness. Jim Cramer's viewers crave financial wellness. But when it comes to the legal wellness bucket, which when it tips, it spills into the previous two because you freak out and go broke, the only content available is those ginned-up courtroom shows that are more exploitative than helpful; the cameras show up after it's too late and the victims' problems have already occurred.

My goal is to turn back the dial and discuss how to *prevent* legal problems in the first place, the way an annual physical helps to keep you from getting sick. That's what legal aptitude, awareness, and wellness are all about. I'll show you how to give yourself a *legal* physical, so you can hopefully stay out of legal trouble entirely or address it effectively should it occur. And by doing so, I hope you'll avoid steep out-of-pocket costs, including an attorney's.

These are the reasons I started my brand, Your Lovable Lawyer, which began with writing, taping, and producing videos in my basement with a green screen and costumes I ordered on (and promptly returned to) Amazon. I grew comfortable taping my YouTube and TikTok videos after thirteen years of chairing our nation's largest, most prominent, and most respected class-action litigation educational program for lawyers, federal judges, and professors—the American Bar Association National Institute on Class Action. (After thirteen years, my wife convinced me nobody at the Institute needed to hear anything more from me!)

While running the Institute, instead of offering vapid, soulless, and antiseptic panel discussions and text-dense PowerPoint presentations that quickly chased attendees to their iPhones, I wrote three-act plays, produced talk shows and game shows, and crafted mock hearings, mock mediations, and other original and memorable content. Why? Because it's all about entertaining people. If you don't do that, it's impossible for learning to occur. I've baked that style and vibe into this book. I took my best and most engaging legal content and wrote it for nonlawyers in a way that entertains while it teaches.

As I hope you're already appreciating, I'm enthusiastic about delivering the law in a fun and friendly way that empowers people and makes them comfortable with and confident about their legal rights. I do this because I know it will improve people's outcomes after companies such as airlines, credit card issuers, and cell phone providers have taken advantage of them.

Simply put, the law is like air—it affects us and permeates everything. There's nothing we can do to avoid it. And because we can't ignore the law, we must learn how to use it to our advantage. This book will give you that power. And to demonstrate how relatable and accessible the legal information I'll share is, I'll channel pretty much all of it through my personal experiences—situations that happened to or involved me, friends, or clients (anonymized as appropriate to protect privilege). Because if these things could happen to us, they could happen to you. And if I was able to get out of them, armed with the legal information I'll share, you can too. Simply put, this book's goal is to add immediate value to your life by cutting out the middle person—the lawyer—and teaching you the importance of standing up for yourself.

Chapter 3
How big business is out to screw you

People will do anything to make money. The drive to make as much of it as possible will never go out of style. If it did, lawyers would be out of business.

But often, making money unjustly comes at the expense of people who can least afford it. People and companies will keep taking and taking and taking until somebody pushes back. And the people pushing back are usually lawyers—often class-action lawyers.

Make no mistake about it, over the past several decades, consumer schemes have proliferated. This is a direct result of technology that has spawned a massive increase in the number of promotional and marketing strategies aimed at consumers. This has led to innumerable discount offers, loyalty programs, email ads, and other incentives that create overwhelming choices for consumers, often resulting in confusion. This avalanche of product offerings (often obliquely via the Internet or mobile apps) has exponentially increased the ways you can get screwed.

Many companies offer multiple variations of a product or a variety of loyalty tiers, coupon types, or promotional channels that require consumers to navigate a complex maze of choices. Fitting this profile are airlines and the way they offer various pricing structures and add-ons, which is made more difficult when booking online or via mobile app, because they charge you to book with a live representative.

Added to this, technology, interconnectivity, 24/7 communication, and increased accessibility have made competition more intense. This pressure-filled landscape has forced companies to differentiate themselves, sometimes insincerely, and peddle various schemes to attract customers.

These new realities often result in unfairness to consumers. We end up confused, unable to understand the deals companies are offering us. I mean, how many times have we been forced to click through pop-up windows to complete a transaction, not knowing what we agreed to or whether we got the best deal?

These relentless marketing ploys and sales tactics lead to "decision fatigue"—a state of mental exhaustion that often leads to poor decision-making. These sales methods can also cause reduced value perception, where consumers perceive a product or service to have less value than it actually does.

Scams and exploitation are a lot more sophisticated than they used to be. They're tougher to detect, tougher to trace, and tougher to prove. They're more prevalent too. Just look at the incoming call feed on your cell phone. You probably get several robocalls per day; this is easily the most popular scam around. (In fact, I got one as I was writing this paragraph!) But as ridiculous as robocalls sound—whether you're being offered a timeshare, a Vegas vacation, or something related to Medicare Part D—if they weren't effective, robocallers wouldn't keep making them.

Robocallers prey on vulnerable people, often the elderly, uneducated, and financially desperate. And their schemes have become a lot more systematized because there's now a lot more money to be made. No longer is a snake oil salesperson steering their wagon through town; these are widescale, often global, schemes.

Sadly, the consequences of falling prey to a robocall scheme are more severe than ever. Victims sometimes provide access to their checking or credit card accounts, or they purchase gift cards and give up the PINs. If you don't recognize the risks, it's only a matter of time before you're the victim of identity theft, credit card fraud, or a drained bank account.

It's because of all the science, analytics, and effort that companies put into maximizing the dollars they squeeze from you that I decided to write this book. It's simply not fair what rich, lawyered-up companies can and will do if left to their own devices. It's time we leveled the playing field. The only way to do that is to become empowered, so you can detect wrongdoing, keep tabs on your legal health, and put a dent into big companies bent on screwing you over. That way, these companies will no longer be able to prey on the vulnerable; instead, they'll find only informed people who are unwilling to be abused anymore.

Chapter 4
The importance of avoiding a victim mentality

Fighting back begins with your state of mind. That means not having a victim mentality. Take, for instance, a friend who recently visited the dentist for a crown. Half an hour after he got home, the crown fell off. Worse yet, not much of his tooth remained.

Out of sorts, he called me because he'd charged this debacle on his credit card—$2,400! He knew he needed to see another dentist and didn't want to double-pay, but he was terrified about calling Visa to contest the first dentist's charge. "What if the dentist sues me?" he pleaded. "What if Visa sides with him? I don't want to cause more trouble." He had a victim mentality.

I tried to reframe the situation for him. "You're concerned about the dentist suing *you*? He oughta be concerned about your suing *him*!" I added, "You have the right to contest a charge with Visa. So hit the dentist where it hurts most—in his wallet." I told my friend he needed to stand up for himself because he was right, and his dentist was wrong. Heck, for all he knew, the dentist would offer to fix his tooth for free or refund his money.

I was confident his dentist would neither contest his credit card reversal nor send his case to collections. Few lawyers would agree to pursue such a small-value claim. I told him that at the end of the day, his dentist just wanted to get paid and—above all—didn't want to get sued in a medical malpractice case. That's the worst thing a doctor can have on their record. Who, I asked him, had the upper hand now?

So my friend did two things: He contested the charge with Visa, and he wrote a professional and factually accurate email (that I tweaked) to the dentist's office, explaining what happened and why he believed it was the dentist's fault. He'd never have taken this tack had he continued to think like a victim instead of like a powerful, enabled, self-aware consumer who knew how to stand up for his legal rights.

After this cognitive shift, my friend told me the skies parted, angels sang, and harps played because he saw his legal health and entitlement to justice in a whole new, glorious way. Ultimately, the dentist's office wrote off the $2,400. And for good measure, another dentist fixed my friend's tooth a few days later for $800 less!

Because the examples are as endless as they are real, here's another. This one involves two friends who'd ordered a leather couch and chair from a major nationwide furniture retailer. When their order arrived, it was all messed up in the manner described in my letter below.

My friends didn't tell me about all this for a couple of weeks. But when they did, I sprang into action. "Your retailer screwed you! You can do something about it, or you can let them get the best of you."

After some modest cajoling—as well as explaining their legal rights and why they had every reason to exert them—my friends accepted my offer to write a letter for them. Here's what it said:

> **<u>Certified Mail, Return Receipt Requested</u>**
>
> Charles Montgomery Burns
> Springfield Nuclear Power Plant—
> Retail Furniture Division
> 3469 Nuclear Drive
> Springfield, OH 45501
>
> RE: Order #60969045349
>
> Dear Mr. Burns [Burns is SNPP's CEO; I sent the same letter to SNPP's general counsel, meaning its chief in-house lawyer],
>
> I represent Marge and Homer Simpson with respect to order #60969045349, placed on October 9, 2021, for a four-piece couch and swivel leather chair. Exhibit 1 (SNPP order confirmation).
>
> The Simpsons are long-time SNPP customers who are generally exceptionally pleased with your products. But on June 3, 2022, that changed. After waiting several months for their order, they were disappointed to discover that one of their modular couch sections was the wrong color, and their swivel leather chair was scuffed in three places. Exhibit 2 (photos of the furniture defects).

On June 8, 2022, my clients' decorator spoke with Mr. Millhouse at SNPP's East Springfield store—the store from which they purchased their furniture. Their decorator described the problems, and Millhouse ordered a replacement couch section. He also offered my clients $300, which he described as a "discount" on the scuffed chair and suggested they put the $300 toward fixing it.

Alternatively, Mr. Millhouse advised that SNPP would offer no discount and would instead remake the chair, which would take several more months. My clients opted for Mr. Millhouse to reorder the chair.

On June 14, 2022, SNPP advised my clients that, due to the global supply-chain disruption, their couch order would be delayed until late December 2022. Exhibit 3 (SNPP order update).

Throughout this process, Ms. Simpson called Mr. Millhouse repeatedly, but he never returned her calls.

All told, SNPP never offered my clients any pricing relief on their couch, and it merely offered $300 off the price of their chair, which they refused in favor of a replacement chair.

SNPP's actions subject it to liability under Ohio and federal law. First, "[a] cause of action for breach of contract requires the claimant to establish the existence of a contract, the failure without legal excuse of the other party to perform when performance is due, and damages or loss resulting from the breach." *Lucarell v. Nationwide Mut. Ins. Co.*, 152 Ohio St. 3d 453, 469 (2018).

My clients contracted for a single-color modular couch and an unscuffed leather chair, but they received neither. They performed their contract with SNPP but have not received the benefit of their bargain.

Additionally, under O.R.C. § 1302.27(A), "a warranty that the goods shall be merchantable is implied in a contract for their sale if the seller is a merchant with respect to goods of that kind." To be merchantable, they "must be at least such as [to] pass without objection in the trade under the contract description…." *Id.* at (B)(1). By any measure, a multicolor couch and scuffed chair do not satisfy this standard.

Finally, the Magnuson-Moss Warranty Act provides that "a consumer who is damaged by the failure of a supplier, warrantor, or service contractor to comply with any obligation under this title, or under a written warranty, implied warranty, or service contract, may bring suit for damages and other legal and equitable relief…." 15 U.S.C. § 2310(d)(1). Similar to the reasons involving my clients' warranty claim, SNPP is liable to them under Magnuson-Moss.

The total price of my clients' contract with SNPP is $6,274.57. To avoid litigation, they demand the following relief:

1. SNPP provide them with a new leather chair, as ordered; they will keep the damaged chair in the meantime. For their inconvenience, SNPP will provide a twenty-five percent refund of the chair's price.
2. SNPP provide them with a twenty-five percent discount toward the total price of the couch and remove the nonconforming section when the conforming section arrives.

Taken together, my clients demand payment of $1,568.64 as full compensation for SNPP malfeasance. I'm happy to discuss their situation, and you can reach me at the above-listed number. If I don't hear from you by July 15, 2022, my clients have instructed me to file suit. But considering their relationship with your company and its reputation for standing behind its products, I'm confident that won't be necessary.

I look forward to your cooperation.

Best personal regards.

Very truly yours,
s/Daniel R. Karon
Daniel R. Karon

As you can see, there was a lot more here than, "I guess we just have to take it." No more than a week after I sent my letter, I received a call from one of the company's associate general counsel. She was just shy of frantic.

"I'm so sorry for what happened to your clients," she said. "We never want anything to escalate to the level where we receive a letter, especially from a lawyer. I'm so sorry your clients' salesperson didn't connect with them. Just tell me what we can do to make this right."

I smiled, knowing my letter had done its job. I explained that the relief my clients sought was right there in the letter. By the time our short conversation ended, the associate general counsel had agreed to provide my clients with everything I demanded. Granted, this incident involved, in part, unavoidable supply-chain issues, but that was neither my clients' concern nor fault. The issue was the wrong-colored couch section and the scuffed chair, the replacement of which would take an extra-long time *because* of the supply-chain issues.

By the time all this ended, the company not only delivered my friends a correctly colored couch section and replacement chair, but it also let them keep the first chair and sent them a check for $1,568.64! It was a win in every sense and for little more than my friends standing up for themselves and channeling their grievances through the law.

That's why I reproduced my entire letter for you. Indeed, I'm going to include lots of letters I wrote for myself and others. These letters demonstrate and address situations we all experience. If you can lift and implement pieces and concepts from my solutions to help solve your own, I'll have done my job.

That said, I'm certainly not suggesting that what I wrote will fit the bill when you have a problem with a retailer or other business. But my ideas and approach could help when you find yourself in a comparable situation, whether with a furniture retailer, car dealership, medical practitioner, or anyone else.

When a company does you dirty, you needn't simply take it. Think critically about whether what happened to you is wrong. If it truly is, the law usually provides a remedy. After all, the law is rooted in the pursuit of fairness and justice.

Companies are made up of people like us. People who get screwed, and people who are just as intimidated by the law as we are. So try to remember who you're talking to. It's not the Wizard of Oz. It's some little guy behind the curtain. If you make a sensible ask based on the facts, often you'll end up getting what you want. This is how you need to look at yourself and the commerce you conduct. You don't want to get steamrolled; you want to be the steamroller.

In law, as in life, the squeaky wheel gets the grease. With that mindset in place, let's dig into some of the most common and aggravating consumer scams and overreaches and discuss how you can push back or, better yet, avoid them in the first place.

Chapter 5
Putting the airlines in their place

A canceled flight can be a good thing—sometimes a *very* good thing—and I'll explain why.

Don't get me wrong, canceled flights stink—big time. Worse still is the runaround that follows. Hours in line or on the phone. Or how about when the call drops after an hour on hold with the airline? And, of course, they never call back. Then, when *you* call back and finally talk to someone, they don't care that you're into hour two of waiting for a solution when *that* call drops. I'm getting aggravated just writing about this!

We pay good money for (often expensive) airline tickets, and we deserve better. But don't expect the airlines to recognize it when you don't get what you pay for. You're only one of millions of travelers. You need to self-advocate. Here's a 100 percent true and unvarnished story involving my wife and me, from which I hope you'll be able to draw comparisons and derive lessons for when you're screwed because if you do any traveling, it *will* happen.

My harrowing travel tale, and how I made the most from it

Recently, we were booked on a nonstop flight to visit my parents over the holidays. We left the house at 6:00 a.m. on the morning of the flight to take our dogs to the kennel. After we dropped them off, I received a text message from the airline indicating our flight was delayed for two hours.

After an hour, I received another text describing another hour-long delay. Things didn't look good, but we didn't receive a message canceling our flight. You know what *that* means—we had to go to the airport. So fighting white-out conditions, we crept our way there. We parked, checked our bags, and passed through security. Then, just as we arrived at our gate, I received another text from the airline: "Canceled."

When we sought to rebook, we learned we couldn't fly out till the day after next. Then, the airline extended *that* flight for another two days, putting us on a connecting flight instead of a nonstop as we'd booked. Plus, the airline gave us separate middle seats for both flights instead of seats together. And because it wasn't fair to our dogs to pick them up only to drop them off again, all this meant two days of unnecessary (and not inexpensive) boarding.

Most people would complain to their partner or friends, shrug their shoulders, and chalk up all this aggravation to the nature of air travel. But not me. This wasn't weather-related; this was *careless*-related. Not only had we been inconvenienced, but we were also out the cost of the extra kennel stay and airport parking, we missed a good chunk of our holiday, we were charged for two nights at an Airbnb that we couldn't enjoy, we had to connect when we were supposed to have a nonstop flight, and we had crappy (and separate) middle seats. None of this was okay.

Because I'm all about self-advocating, the squeaky wheel getting the grease, and not having a victim mentality (as well as knowing all about the Department of Transportation's Passenger Bill of Rights,[1] which I'll get to in a bit), I took matters into my own hands. I wrote a very respectful letter. My wife and I were separate travelers, so I could have written two letters, fearing the airline could collapse the relief I requested into a single payment. But because I'd successfully written combined letters to this airline before, I didn't feel the need to double my work.

In my letter, I didn't threaten to sue the airline, and I didn't accuse it of being the worst airline ever. I simply explained what happened in a way that I thought would evoke emotion and empathy. After setting the table and listing my out-of-pocket costs, I made my sensible and well-supported ask: out-of-pocket expense reimbursement and a $1,000 travel voucher for each of us. I supported both asks with itineraries, boarding passes, and receipts. Not only did documentation make me look like a serious advocate, but it also proved that everything I said was 100 percent true, which is the only kind of truth I know.

Importantly, I didn't submit this request through the airline's customer service portal. If I've learned anything in thirty-four years of practice it's that letters—yes, old-school letters—get stamped "received," get read, and, importantly, can't be deleted. I sent a letter not only to customer service but also to the airline's CEO and chief legal counsel. I sent them Certified Mail, "Return Receipt Requested," so I would know the airline got my letters, and the airline would know I knew.

1 https://www.transportation.gov/airconsumer.

As I hoped, a week later, I received two emails from customer service. The first read, "We apologize for the inconvenience you experienced on your recent trip. We have issued a $500.00 electronic travel certificate to Daniel Karon, valid toward the purchase of airline tickets on eligible flights.... Thank you and we look forward to welcoming you on board again soon." The second email was identical, except it awarded the $500 electronic travel certificate to my wife. Separate from these emails, I received a check for my out-of-pocket expenses.

This whole time, I knew $1,000 wasn't going to happen. But I've also learned in my business that you need to aim high. Had I requested $500, the airline would have likely offered us only $100. The airline's offer satisfied us, and I'd like to think everyone involved in this transaction walked away comfortable and satisfied they did the right thing. This is the type of outcome you deserve, too.

To bring this story to life—and provide you with concrete thoughts and insights for when you craft your inevitable airline letter—here's my actual letter. Take a look, and we'll discuss it afterward.

Via Certified Mail, Return Receipt Requested and email to customercareandfeedback@centralperk.com and centralperk.com/feedback

Monica Geller, CEO
Chandler Bing, Chief Legal Counsel
Central Perk Airlines
199 Lafayette St.
New York, NY 10012

RE: Daniel Karon AirMiles Premium Account Number: RX349584
Miriam Karon AirMiles Premium Account Number: PS455960
Original Date of Travel: December 23, 2022
Confirmation Numbers: KTR485 (Daniel Karon), FUE832 (Miriam Karon)

Dear Ms. Geller and Mr. Bing,

Typically, we enjoy our travel on Central Perk Airlines and are quick to compliment the many good employees who make our travel seamless—even sending laudatory messages. But our most recent travel experience was anything but pleasant. It ruined the holidays and time with my aging parents and resulted in distress and out-of-pocket expenses. And while we understand the weather challenges that occurred this holiday season, the challenges I'll describe did not relate to the weather.

On December 23, we arrived early at Cleveland Hopkins Airport for our nonstop flight to Phoenix. (Exhibit A) Central Perk delayed our departure time to account for the weather. Only after we arrived at the gate did Central Perk cancel our flight, which, given the weather, was frustrating but understandable. Central Perk rebooked us on a nonstop flight on December 25.

During the twenty-four hours leading up to our December 25 flight, I repeatedly attempted to check in on the Central Perk app and website, but neither would permit us. Accordingly, we arrived at Hopkins Airport over ninety minutes before flight time to check in at the kiosk.

When the kiosk refused to cooperate, we approached the ticket counter. The agent told us you had released our seats because we allegedly hadn't checked in ahead of time (ninety minutes remained till departure), and no nonstop seats to Phoenix were available till December 28.

Not only did Central Perk's lack of functionality prevent us from checking in for our December 25 flight, but we also arrived well ahead of departure to check in. The ticket agent explained that Central Perk had mistakenly given away our seats and refused to retrieve them because the recipients had already received their boarding passes. As a result, we were left scrambling for flights to see my parents.

Eventually, the agent found availability through O'Hare on December 27 with a long layover that didn't put us into Phoenix until late that night. But our Cleveland-O'Hare flight was delayed due to operational issues, and our O'Hare-Phoenix flight ended up delayed due to operational issues, too. What's more, we were assigned separate middle seats for both segments instead of seats together, as we had booked.

This delay caused us to arrive so late that we needed to take an Uber, which resulted in an additional unexpected cost of $39.14 (Exhibit D). Our daughter, whom we had not seen in months, arrived two days before we did, and our time seeing her was cut considerably shorter than had only the weather intervened.

We take no issue with our travel irregularities due to the weather and commend Central Perk for suitably handling these challenges, including a wonderful on-phone experience we had with Rachel Green at your Minneapolis call center. It's your app's and website's lack of functionality, coupled with giving away our seats—after we'd already lost two days with our daughter and my parents—that, as even the Cleveland ticketing desk agent admitted, was inexcusable.

Because of Central Perk's carelessness (and *not* due to the weather), we suffered the following out-of-pocket damages:

- Two days of unused and unrefunded Airbnb: $382.29 (Exhibit B).
- Two days of unnecessary dog-sitting (it was impractical and cruel to retrieve our dogs for such a short time): $200 (Exhibit C).
- Uber: $39.14 (Exhibit D)

- One hour of parking on December 25, 2022, when we unnecessarily arrived for the flight: $15 (Exhibit E).

In addition to these damages, we made three trips to the airport and spent several frustrating hours on the phone sorting out the travel issue that Central Perk—not the weather—caused us. I hope you'd agree that Central Perk should not treat premium travelers this way, and we shouldn't have had to spend so much time sorting out Central Perk's avoidable operational problems. For these inconveniences, we request the following relief:

- $1,000 travel voucher for Daniel Karon
- $1,000 travel voucher for Miriam Karon

Taken together, our out-of-pocket expenses total $636.43, which we request in addition to our respective $1,000 travel vouchers.

Like you, we are sorry for our troubling Central Perk experience, and we thank you for your understanding. We have always been loyal to Central Perk Airlines and are confident that Central Perk will demonstrate its loyalty to us.

Best personal regards and very Happy Holidays.

Very truly yours,
s/Daniel R. Karon
Daniel R. Karon

That was my honest-to-goodness letter to the airlines with names changed to protect the guilty. Notice a few important things (or "elements," as lawyers call them):

1. I used the sandwich technique. That means starting out nice ("Typically, we enjoy our travel on Central Perk Airlines and are quick to compliment the many good employees who make our travel seamless...."), followed by the problem ("But our most recent travel experience was anything but pleasant."), and finishing nicely ("Like you, we are sorry for our troubling Central Perk experience, and we thank you for your understanding."). Take another look at my SNPP-furniture letter. You'll see I employed this technique there, too.
2. Notice I included all my documents (or "evidence"), so I'm not *telling* the airline the facts—I'm *showing* the airline the facts. Showing, not telling, is the hallmark of good legal—indeed, *any*—writing. If you tell them, they won't believe you, but if you *show* them, they'll have no choice but to agree.
3. My ask is highly specific, including exact dollar amounts. After all, if you don't ask, you don't get.
4. I addressed the airline's defense: the weather. You want your opponent to know you're on to them. This way, when they figure, "We can just blame it on the weather," they'll know that excuse won't fly (so to speak).
5. Throw in a compliment or two; it makes you look good ("We take no issue with our travel irregularities due to the weather and commend Central Perk for suitably handling these challenges [as well as the] wonderful on-phone experience we had with Rachel Green at your Minneapolis call center.").

6. Evoke the reader's sympathy. This persuasive technique—also described as pathos—derives from Aristotle's *Art of Rhetoric* and is a tried-and-true method for moving an opponent toward your position.
7. Aim high. You'll see my slightly (but not too) high travel voucher asks. Whatever you request, your opponent is sure to offer you less. So be sure to aim high enough that you allow yourself to emerge from the negotiation happy but not so high that you turn off the other side. Requesting $1,000 seemed sensible, and my wife and I agreed beforehand we'd be happy with travel vouchers of $200 or more. Experience negotiating with your vendors will help you to decide where your sweet spot is.

Instead of simply including my letter, I've "annotated" it for you, meaning I broke it down. This way, you can understand precisely how and why I crafted it as I did. (I showed, not told, you—get it?) And though my letter (and others throughout this book) has a ton of elements baked into it, you won't necessarily need to include all of them in *your* eventual letter. Indeed, perhaps you'll come up with additional elements you'll use instead. My goal is to spark your thinking and creativity, so you'll be able to fire off something like this—on your terms, based on your facts—when the airlines or others stick it to you.

And if you're wondering about the result, the airline sent us each $500 travel vouchers. This surpassed the $200 each we'd hoped for; plus, the airline accounted for almost 100 percent of our out-of-pocket expenses. A pretty darn good result!

The Department of Transportation's got your back

Earlier, I mentioned the Department of Transportation's Passenger Bill of Rights. It provides several things that favor you so feel free to blend them into any letter you write.

For example, according to the Passenger Bill of Rights, US airlines operating domestic and international flights must provide passengers with food and water no later than two hours after the beginning of a tarmac delay. While the aircraft sits on the tarmac, lavatories must remain operable, and medical attention must be available if needed. We've all heard *those* nightmares.

Also, overbooking flights isn't illegal. Most airlines overbook their scheduled flights to compensate for no-shows. As a result, you could end up getting bumped. When an oversale occurs, airlines must ask passengers whether they'd like to give up their seats in exchange for compensation. No problem here. It's when you're bumped *against* your will that you're entitled to compensation—compensation you need to know you're entitled to seek if the airline doesn't offer it.

The Passenger Bill of Rights requires all airlines to give passengers who are bumped involuntarily a written statement describing their rights and explaining how the airline decides who gets on an oversold flight and who doesn't. If you don't make the cut, you're entitled to a check or cash as denied-boarding compensation.

The minimum amount depends on the price of your ticket and the length of the delay. Department of Transportation requirements describe the minimum, but airlines may choose to provide a higher amount. If you believe you deserve more than the airline is willing to give, now you know how to write them a letter.

Here are some particulars from the Passenger Bill of Rights you might not know to demand. For as we all know, if you don't ask, you don't get:

- If the airline bumps you involuntarily yet arranges substitute transportation that gets you to your destination within an hour of your original scheduled arrival time, you're not entitled to compensation.
- But if the airline arranges substitute transportation that gets you to your destination between one and two hours after your original arrival time (and between one and four hours on international flights), the airline must pay you at least 200 percent of your one-way fare to your final destination that day or $1,075, whichever is less.
- If the substitute transportation is scheduled to get you to your destination more than two hours later (and four hours internationally), or if the airline doesn't make substitute travel arrangements for you, the minimum compensation doubles to 400 percent of your one-way fare or $2,150, whichever is less.
- If your ticket does not indicate a fare (for example, you bought with miles), your denied boarding compensation is based on the lowest payment charged for a ticket in the same class of service (meaning, coach, premium, or first class) on that flight.
- If you paid for seat selection or checked baggage on your original flight and you didn't receive those services on your substitute flight or had to pay a second

time, the airline that bumped you must refund you those payments.

That's a whole lot on delayed and canceled flights and the possible need to fashion your request for compensation into a letter, especially if your situation raised one of the above issues. (By the way, I mailed my letter before the Department of Transportation amended the Passenger Bill of Rights to include the preceding relief. That's why my letter doesn't refer to it.)

Now let's turn to everybody's second least favorite airline problem: luggage. Luggage problems fall into three categories, and the airline's responsibility to you depends on what happened.

Damaged luggage

Here's the sitch according to the Passenger Bill of Rights—rights you need to have handy when airport personnel claim ignorance, which you *know* will happen.

If your suitcase arrives smashed or torn, the airline must pay to repair it. If it's unfixable, the airline must offer to pay you its depreciated value. The problem there is that half the cost of your suitcase won't buy you a new suitcase. So what do you do? You advocate using the same techniques in my letter to address your damaged suitcase. Appeal to justice and fairness because, remember, a real person is reading your letter.

This same approach applies to the things you pack inside your suitcase. If something breaks, the airline could refuse to pay, insisting it was poorly packed and therefore your fault. The airline could also refuse to pay you for damaged items because your suitcase is undamaged.

If you packed your things well and truly believe the airline is at fault for breaking something, explain why and go after what you deserve. Again (and as always), there's nothing preventing you from standing up for yourself in a manner that too few passengers do and politely asking for (not demanding) what you deserve. There's no harm in asking, and the worst thing the airline can say is "no." (Of course, if they say "no," the journey needn't end there. Read on…)

Delayed luggage

We've all waited with dread as the bags rolling onto the conveyor belt dwindle. Then, the belt stops, and we're left standing at baggage claim alone—the unlucky flier.

A few years ago, this happened to my wife and mother-in-law on a flight to Brussels to visit our daughter, who was studying abroad. After two days of travel that involved missed flights and delays, they finally arrived in Brussels, but their bags didn't. To make matters worse, it was a weekend, meaning very few stores were open. This made it extremely difficult for them to purchase necessities. And, of course, all of this was against the backdrop of wondering whether their luggage would even arrive at all.

Yes, delayed luggage is a huge inconvenience but don't panic. Airlines have sophisticated systems to track down your missing bags, often returning them to you within hours. Plus, airlines will often offer to pay you for reasonable expenses you incur while they look for your bags. That said, you and your airline might have different ideas about what's reasonable. That's where I come in.

But first things first. If your bags don't come off the conveyor belt, go straight to baggage services and report it. Insist that they create a report and give you a copy, even if they claim your bag will be on the next flight. (Famous last words!) Be sure to get a phone number to follow up. And I don't mean through the airline's main reservations number; get the number that rings directly into the little office in the baggage claim area. And don't assume the airline will deliver your bag without charge when they find it. Be sure to ask whether there's a charge. If they tell you there is, demand they waive it.

Though I've never seen this next point in action, the Department of Transportation claims most airlines have guidelines allowing airport employees to disburse money for emergency purchases. If the airline fails to offer a cash advance, it needs to reimburse you later.

When you need to replace clothing or other items (as my wife and mother-in-law did), the airline might offer to pay you only a portion of what you paid, claiming you'll be able to use the new items even after the originals are returned or that you took advantage of the airline's credit card. To this, I say, "No dice!" Just because you end up with a new shirt doesn't mean you needed one. Don't fall for this chintzy ploy. To me, that's too cute by half.

Airlines are responsible for provable damages up to the amount of their liability limit—$4,700 for domestic flights, regulated by the Department of Transportation and adjusted for inflation every two years. If you can't resolve your claim with the airline's airport staff, keep a record of the names of the employees you worked with and keep all of your travel documents (boarding passes and itineraries) and receipts. You'll need all these materials for your letter.

Lost luggage

Days have passed, and the airline has declared your bag lost. If your flight involves a connection, the last airline is usually responsible for processing your claim even if you believe another airline lost your bag.

To start, don't exaggerate your claim. Airlines have been there, they've done that, and they're good at sniffing out such schemes. If you put a bad taste in the airline's mouth, it could affect how they handle your claim. But don't think acting fairly and honestly will automatically get you what you deserve. Instead, the airline will estimate the value of your lost items, offering to pay what *it* thinks it owes you. If this sounds like how insurance companies treat you, you're right. The airlines will offer to pay your articles' depreciated value, not their original price or replacement cost, as if you want a pair of used pants to replace your new pair.

Though the airline will request receipts and other documentation to back up claims, it's common not to have any of that stuff. After all, if an airline lost my favorite pair of jeans, I could neither tell you where I got them nor how much they cost.

In this instance, you'll have to negotiate and advocate, but don't expect the airline to be your friend. And when you engage the airline, be sure to do so in writing, whether by letter (preferably) or email (for shorter messages). You'll want a record of each interaction. If you need to take the airline to small claims court, you'll want exhibits to document your claim.

Though the airlines have systems and protocols to assist you when they damage, delay, or lose your luggage, my experience is that these processes aren't user-friendly. My experience is also that you can't expect to get back the maximum you deserve without self-advocating.

Thinking the airline will automatically and always do for you what the Passenger Bill of Rights sets out is aspirational at best and fanciful at worst. I've never had a delay, cancellation, or luggage issue resolve organically—as in the airline saw fit to take care of me out of the goodness of its heart. I've *always* needed to self-advocate, despite the systems presumably in place to help me. And now that you know how the airlines operate and have a template for making those operations work to your advantage, you should be in good shape to take control of your dispute.

Again, it comes back to writing the airline and demanding what you want. And when you write your letter, knowing what's happening under the airline's hood will teach you what to expect and where to push and prod to get what you deserve. Because make no mistake, you cannot rely on the airlines to take care of you. You're the only one who can take care of yourself and your family.

Let me wrap up the luggage discussion with the letter I wrote in response to my wife and mother-in-law's delayed luggage debacle:

> **Via Certified Mail, Return Receipt Requested and email to customercareandfeedback@centralperk.com and centralperk.com/feedback**
>
> Monica Geller, CEO
> Chandler Bing, Chief Legal Counsel
> Central Perk Airlines
> 199 Lafayette St.
> New York, NY 10012

RE: Miriam Karon AirMiles Premium Account Number: PS455960
Nancy Friedman AirMiles Frequent-Traveler Account Number DF593877
Original Date of Travel: October 17, 2019
Confirmation Numbers: KX34JJ (Miriam Karon), S8RR82 (Nancy Friedman)

Dear Ms. Geller and Mr. Bing,

I'm writing on behalf of my wife and mother-in-law, loyal Central Perk Airlines flyers. Typically, they enjoy effortless travel with your top-flight airline. But I'm sorry to advise you that their most recent journey fell dramatically short of their expectations.

Recently, my wife took her eighty-five-year-old mother to visit our daughter, who was studying in Brussels for the semester. Their flight from Cleveland connected through O'Hare, and they each checked one bag. *See* Group Exhibit A (boarding passes from CLE to ORD) and Group Exhibit B (baggage claim tickets).

Due to mechanical issues, their flight left late from Cleveland, though the captain did her best to make up for lost time. Her efforts provided them with only forty-five minutes to make it to their connecting gate. Thing is, they arrived at gate C32, but their connection to Brussels through Frankfurt departed from gate E8. *See* Group Exhibit C (boarding passes from

ORD to FRA). And though at least thirty minutes were available to connect (your domestic layover policy), I suspect you would agree that even the most able-bodied passenger could not have made this almost mile-long connection at O'Hare, especially when also considering the time required to deplane.

Not surprisingly, my wife and mother-in-law did not make their connection. They weren't even close. So they were stuck staying at an O'Hare Airport hotel. Yet they could not claim their checked bags. Indeed, they saw their bags locked in the cage at baggage claim, but the baggage personnel refused to release them, despite my wife and mother-in-law needing their toiletries and the lack of anywhere to purchase new ones.

Central Perk rebooked them on a 6:00 a.m. flight, which meant, after arriving at their subpar hotel close to midnight that the airline paid for, they needed to wake up at 4:00 a.m. and return to the airport where they had to suffer through another excruciating security line.

Again, their new itinerary was not nonstop from O'Hare. After dealing with another delay in Frankfurt, they finally arrived in Brussels. But their luggage didn't. They now had only three days left on their trip, and it was the weekend, meaning nowhere was open to purchase the toiletries and clothing they lacked. Come Monday, they purchased what they needed for the next two days. Later on Monday, their bags arrived.

On account of this series of mishaps spawned by Central Perk's mechanical issues, not the weather, my wife and mother-in-law respectfully request Central Perk provide them with the following:

Miriam's damages

- $219.63 for clothing—*see* Group Exhibit D
- $37.43 for toiletries—*see* Group Exhibit E

Nancy's damages

- $165.65 for clothing—*see* Group Exhibit F
- $15.23 for toiletries—*see* Group Exhibit G

In addition to these hard costs proximately caused by Central Perk's failure to perform as expected and required, my wife and mother-in-law each request $1,000 travel certificates for the inconvenience and distress Central Perk put them through. They have been loyal flyers for several years, and they hope you will show them the same commitment and dedication.

Thank you for otherwise seamless travel, and they look forward to Central Perk stepping up, owning this situation, and providing them the requested relief.

Best personal regards.

Very truly yours,
s/Daniel R. Karon
Daniel R. Karon

Notice I didn't cite any law. I didn't need to. I merely told a story, referred to the airline's unfairness, which is what triggers a legal discussion on their end, and made my respectful ask—all while embracing the sandwich technique.

I could have gotten hypertechnical and cited the European Union regulations relating to European travel, but that's a pretty deep dive. Still, if that's someplace you'd like to go (because the regulations are quite generous), go there.

Instead, I chose to be approachable and lay out the facts, channeled through common sense and fairness. Often, that's all you need because, again, the law derives from common sense and fairness anyway.

So how did things turn out? I got my wife and mother-in-law everything I requested, which included the $1,000 transferable travel certificates. And I emphasize *transferable* because when everything was said and done, my mother-in-law gave me her travel certificate, and my wife and I took a free trip to Paris.

You now have a nicely stocked toolbox to draw from when the airlines act up. The approach I've explained resembles the approach lawyers take to writing a legal memo when evaluating a new lawsuit: Issue (lost luggage, canceled flight, or whatever), rule (the Passenger Bill of Rights, the European Union regulations, or simply that you deserve to be treated fairly), analysis (channel the facts through the rule—because you treated me wrongly, my luggage was damaged, I missed my connection and the wedding I was going to, or whatever), and conclusion (your ask—hard costs back plus something for your troubles such as miles or a travel certificate).

This process isn't anything for which you need a lawyer. Again, if you don't ask, you don't get (indeed, asking got my wife and me a free trip to Paris!), so ask with confidence. A little legal awareness, commitment, and elbow grease can often get you a great result.

Contacting the Department of Transportation

Sometimes you don't want compensation or compensation is inappropriate. Sometimes you just want to bitch. If that's your vibe, you can send your airline complaints to the Department of Transportation's Office of Aviation Consumer Protection. You can call, write, or use the Department of Transportation's web-based complaint form.

You may call the Department of Transportation at (202) 366-2220 to describe a consumer-related problem, but if you want the Department of Transportation to process your case as a complaint, you'll need to submit it in writing to this address:

> Office of Aviation Consumer Protection
> US Department of Transportation
> 1200 New Jersey Ave SE
> Washington, DC 20590

Be sure to include your address and phone number along with a complete description of your problem. Use the Department of Transportation's web form to send a complaint electronically.

Consumer complaints help the Department of Transportation spot problems and trends in the airline industry.

Together, consumers provide millions of eyes and ears, and the Department of Transportation takes our complaints seriously.

Indeed, consumer complaints can form the basis for a Department of Transportation enforcement action. Every month, the Department of Transportation publishes a report with information about the number of complaints received about each airline and its problems. You can find this data on the Department of Transportation's website at Air Travel Consumer Report.

The Department of Transportation's website also includes flight delay, oversales, and mishandled baggage statistics. This information could help you choose the more responsible airline, thus sparing you from the possibility of inconvenience.

Stepping things up, if your complaint is about something you believe might be a safety hazard, you may write to the Federal Aviation Administration at this address:

Federal Aviation Administration
Aviation Safety Hotline, AAI-3
800 Independence Ave SW
Washington, DC 20591

You can also call the Federal Aviation Administration at (866) TELL-FAA.

Finally, you may address questions or concerns about security to the Transportation Security Administration as follows:

Transportation Security Administration
601 South 12th St
Arlington, VA 20598
(866) 289-9673

TSA-ContactCenter@dhs.gov

When all else fails, take 'em to court

If nothing works—your email gets ignored, your phone calls fail, or your certified letter and exhibits fall flat—you can always take the airline to small claims court.

Counties nationwide have small claims courts that handle modest-value claims, meaning up to a few thousand dollars, which is often more than your airline-related claim is worth. Jurisdiction will exist in the venue from which your flight departed, meaning you won't have to travel to court—the airline will.

Plus, small claims courts tend to be consumer-friendly, and they employ helpful clerical staff. After all, the staff knows the claimants don't have a legal background. That's why you can often initiate a small claim with just a short, written statement instead of a detailed complaint.

What's more, the cost to initiate a small claim is low. But the real kicker is once you file your quick-and-cheap small claim, the airline needs to take it seriously, which means hiring an expensive lawyer who'll bill the airline several hundred dollars per hour.

This means preparation time and commuting to small claims court will likely eclipse (by a lot) the value of your claim. And because airlines are businesses, they always do the math and often conclude it's easier to pay you than to fight you—even if they think they'll win. (More on the mechanics of small claims court in Chapter 20.)

While your grievance might be low value, maybe the same thing happened to thousands or millions of other travelers. Take, for instance, a Supreme Court case I worked on several years ago involving an airline's decision to bump up frequent flyer members' qualification for a free flight from 20,000 miles to 25,000 miles, despite having promised via its frequent flyer contract to award members a free flight at 20,000 miles. Our client was at 19,000 miles and change when the switch occurred, which meant the free trip he was planning wasn't going to happen for a while longer.

Though my client's damages were slight (he had to accrue an additional 5,000 miles to get the free flight the airline promised him) and surely supported a case in small claims court, we turned it into a class action on behalf of everyone affected by the airline's bait-and-switch. After the airline fought us all the way to the US Supreme Court, where we won, we settled for several million dollars. (More on the mechanics of class actions in Chapter 21.)

But be careful not to go too far

Before you get the idea that it's open season on the airlines and you should complain about every little thing, you need to hear the story of Rabbi S. Binyomin Ginsberg, whose case against Northwest Airlines also wound up before the US Supreme Court.

Ginsberg was a Platinum Elite member of Northwest Airlines' WorldPerks frequent flier program. Platinum Elite was Northwest's highest reward level. But Ginsberg didn't merely fly a lot. He also complained a lot, contacting Northwest twenty-four times in just over six months. Every time, he sought compensation for one reason or another. When Northwest had had enough, it sent him this letter:

> [Y]ou have contacted our office 24 times since December 3, 2007[,] regarding travel problems, including 9 incidents of your bag arriving late at the luggage carousel....Since December 3, 2007, you have continually asked for compensation over and above our guidelines. We have awarded you $1,925.00 in travel credit vouchers, 78,500 WorldPerks bonus miles, a voucher extension for your son, and $491.00 in cash reimbursements....Due to our past generosity, we must respectfully advise that we will no longer be awarding you compensation each time you contact us.
>
> *Northwest, Inc. v. Ginsberg*, 572 U.S. 273, 277–78 (2014).

When Ginsberg requested clarification of his reward status, a Northwest representative sent him an e-mail simply stating that "[a]fter numerous conversations with not only the Legal Department, but with members of the WorldPerks department, I believe your status with the program should be very clear." *Id.* at 278.

Never mind that Northwest's WorldPerks agreement might have been a bit vague, Northwest had had enough. It terminated Ginsberg's WorldPerks membership in keeping with the agreement's language that gave Northwest sole discretion to determine whether a participant had abused the program:

"Northwest terminated [Ginsberg's] membership, apparently in reliance on a provision of the WorldPerks agreement that provided that '[a]buse of the...program (including...improper conduct as determined by [Northwest] in its sole judgment)... may result in cancellation of the member's account.'" *Id.* at 277.

Not surprisingly, Ginsberg didn't take Northwest's response sitting down. He sued Northwest, claiming it terminated his membership in an attempt to cut costs related to its 2008 merger with Delta. His complaint alleged claims for breach of contract, negligent and intentional misrepresentation, and violation of the implied covenant of good faith and fair dealing. But the district court (the initial court where he filed his complaint) dismissed everything. Ginsberg appealed the court's order dismissing his complaint but only his claim for breach of the duty of good faith and fair dealing.

When his case made its way to the Supreme Court, the Court had to decide whether the Airline Deregulation Act of 1978 preempted (meaning killed) his claim because Ginsberg attempted to "enact or enforce a law, regulation, or other provision having the force and effect of law related to a price, route, or service of an air carrier," *id.* at 280, which activities the ADA reserved exclusively for the federal government.

Considering the ADA's language and legislative history (meaning what Congress intended when enacting it), the Court had little difficulty concluding that the ADA preemption provision covered Ginsberg's claim for breach of the duty of good faith and fair dealing.

The Court next considered whether an airline's frequent flier programs relate to its "rates, routes, or services." Answering this question in the affirmative, the Court ruled that the ADA's preemption provisions also applied to Ginsberg's claim.

The Court concluded that Northwest's WorldPerks program was connected to its "rates" because members could earn miles for tickets or seat upgrades that effectively reduced or eliminated the price of a ticket or upgrade.

Finally, the Court added, Northwest's WorldPerks program was connected to "services," because customers could use miles earned through the program to gain "access to flights and to higher service categories."

I could take you on a much deeper dive into federal preemption law, but I won't because what I've described makes my point: If you're a pain in the airlines' neck, they can kick you out of their frequent-flier program and gut your account, and there's basically nothing you can do about it. So while the squeaky wheel tends to get the grease, a wheel that squeaks too much could get kicked out of its airline's frequent flier program.

The Ginsburg case is precisely why I suggest a respectful ask instead of a nasty one. Granted, there's the Passenger Bill of Rights, but we both know that could take forever and a day to implement. So it's your job to get the airlines to feel bad for you and like you at the same time. But you also need to decide how many trips to the well are too many.

Despite all I've said, I'm not a travel scrooge!

From all I've written, you might think I have it out for the airlines—that I'm just an airline crab who does nothing but complain. That's actually not the case. You'll remember from my letter opening this chapter that I'm just as eager to commend the airlines for a job well done, because I think it's essential to be balanced and to give credit where it's due.

To prove my point, here's a letter I sent that you can consider when you decide to make someone's day better because they made yours that way:

Edith Bunker
Archie Airlines
Baggage Service Center
704 Hauser St
Queens, NY 11385

RE: Platinum Account Number: TD563453
Date of Travel: April 11, 2016
Confirmation Number: SA458677

Dear Ms. Bunker:

I felt compelled to write to you concerning George Jefferson's wonderful service concerning our lost baggage claim.

My family and I had just returned from San Francisco, and all but one bag made the connecting flight to Cleveland. As bad luck would have it, the missing bag contained our daughter's clothing and personal items along with her favorite stuffed animal, which she thought she'd never see again.

After being bounced between several customer service agents, I was fortunate to be transferred to Mr. Jefferson, who went out of his way to pursue our missing bag, going so far as to call me multiple times with updates. The good news is that, due largely to his efforts, you found our missing bag and delivered it last week, whereupon I tucked my daughter's stuffed animal safely under her arm as she slept.

> You are lucky to have Mr. Jefferson among your ranks, and we're lucky to have worked with him. I hope you recognize his exceptional customer service as we did.
>
> Best personal regards.
>
> Very truly yours,
> *s/Daniel R. Karon*
> Daniel R. Karon

And if you think such letters go unnoticed or are lost on the airlines, check out the airline's response:

> Hi Daniel,
>
> Thanks so much for your compliment!
>
> I'm happy to hear about the excellent service you received and will pass along your kind words to my co-worker George and his supervisor. I'm sure they will find your gesture meaningful.
>
> We appreciate your business and loyalty and look forward to seeing you on your next getaway.
>
> Warm regards,
> *Gloria*
> Customer Service

Travel can range anywhere from a seamless joyride to a miserable nuisance. When airlines fall short, it's important to step up and avoid getting stepped on. But be thoughtful, state a compelling case that evokes the reader's sympathy, and make a reasonable ask. If you utilize these guidelines, I think you'll be surprised by what you can end up with for your troubles.

Chapter 6
How to detect and avoid travel scams

Unlike most products, travel services usually have to be paid for before they are delivered. This creates opportunities for disreputable people and companies. Some travel packages, for example, turn out to be very different from what was presented or what you expected. Some don't materialize at all.

I'm sure you know what I'm talking about. The phone call about unused travel credits that you can redeem (along with a free trip to Vegas, of course) so long as you provide your credit card number to guarantee it. Or the robocall (we'll get to robocallers in Chapter 13) where a prerecorded voice message claims it's calling you with an exclusive offer from [insert hotel, resort, or cruise line here], adding that your phone number has been preselected to receive a complimentary five-star stay or cruise.

And these scammers are good. I'll admit to having hung in there for several minutes till they requested my credit card. I just *had* to learn how much I was getting for nothing.

But travel scams don't only occur over the telephone. They're rampant online. Third-party scams can be especially dangerous. Let's say you're looking for a vacation rental. The trustworthy sites—Airbnb and VRBO—don't have anything in your price range, so you search further to find a third-party booking site you've never heard of. And boy, are the deals great. But it's not unheard of to arrive at your supposed vacation rental to find no vacation rental, either because you've not rented it, or it just doesn't exist.

That's why you need to be extremely careful before paying and relying on one of these sites. For instance, a few years ago, I had work in Miami and wanted my wife to join me. The trip coincided with our thirtieth wedding anniversary, so I wanted to book someplace nice in Miami Beach.

But it was high season, and none of the trustworthy hotel-booking sites—Expedia, Hotels.com, and the like—offered anything I could afford. (The same experience could have happened with a vacation-rental site.) Then, I stumbled across a hotel-booking site I'd never heard of, and did it ever have great deals! My eyes went right toward a hotel that should have cost around $800 per night, but the website advertised it for $250 per night.

I wasn't so much concerned about giving my credit card number (because I could always contest the charge) as I was about showing up at the property and having no room. Happy anniversary!

So I researched credible travel sites to see what they said about this unfamiliar brand. For all I knew, the brand had a great reputation and had been around for years. Just because *I* hadn't heard of it didn't mean it was all wet.

By the time I finished my research, I'd learned several good things about this website. I comfortably and confidently booked the room, thrilled with the deal I'd gotten. I'm happy to report that the trip went great. In fact, when I told the front desk attendant it was our anniversary (although my wife begged me not to play the anniversary card), he upgraded us to a suite. Happy Anniversary, indeed!

When you receive that offer by phone (or mail) for a free or extremely low-priced trip to a popular destination (often Vegas, Hawaii, or Florida), here are a few things you should ask yourself:

- Does the price seem too good to be true? If so, it probably is.
- Are you being pressured to make an immediate decision?
- Is the carrier simply identified as "a major airline"?
- Does the representative offer you a list of airlines without saying which one you'll be on?
- Is the representative unable or unwilling to give you a street address for the company?
- Does the representative say you can't leave for at least two months? (The federal legal deadline for disputing a credit card charge is sixty days, and most scam artists know this.)

If you answered "yes" to any of these red flags, proceed with caution. Ask for written information to be sent to you; any legitimate travel company will gladly oblige. Don't trust their website—everybody has a splashy one. If they don't have a brochure, ask for a day or two to think it over; most bona fide deals that are good today will still be good two days from now. If they say no to these requests, this probably isn't the trip for you.

The list of things to look out for is endless, but here are some more big ones:

- If you are told you've won a free vacation, ask if you have to buy something else to get it. Some packages promote free airfare, so long as you buy an expensive hotel room. Others include a free hotel stay but no airfare.
- If you are seriously considering the vacation offer and are confident you have established the full price you'll pay, compare it to what you might get through the popular booking sites. Often, the allure of free airfare or free accommodations disguises the fact that you're overpaying for your trip.
- Get a confirmed departure date in writing before you pay anything. Skeptically view any promises that you can arrange an acceptable date later. If the package involves standby or waitlist travel or a reservation that can only be provided much later, ask if your payment is refundable if you want to cancel, and don't pay any money you can't afford to lose.
- If the destination is a beach resort, ask the seller how far the hotel is from the beach. Then ask the hotel.
- Determine the complete cost of the trip in dollars, including all service charges, taxes, processing fees, etc.
- If you decide to buy the trip after checking it out, paying by credit card gives you the legal right to pursue a chargeback (credit) if the booker doesn't deliver promised services.

Vacations are supposed to be fun, not a field day for scammers. Be smarter than they are and don't walk into trouble. Do your homework so you can confidently travel and have the fun you deserve.

Chapter 7
How to protect yourself when you're in an auto accident

Auto accidents happen every day, and they're scary. Sometimes they're your fault; sometimes they're someone else's. And fault—or at least your belief as to who's at fault—can radically affect how you need to behave, including what you say to whom, if anyone.

And never mind what you see on TV—the truth is that insurance companies *don't* care about you, and they *don't* want to pay you. In fact, did you know insurance companies routinely deny coverage to their insureds (meaning you!), sometimes going so far as to file insurance-coverage lawsuits where they ask a court to rule that they *don't* owe coverage? Yep, all this for having dutifully paid your insurance premiums. (Just wait—the next chapter is all about coverage denial!)

So just how do insurance companies respond following an auto accident? You might receive a call from the other driver's claims adjuster, asking what happened. Often, that adjuster's goal is to walk you into an admission that the accident was your fault—all while recording your conversation. And in most states, recording a conversation is legal so long as one party (here, the claims adjuster) knows the recording is occurring. *See, e.g., People v. Lasher*, 58 N.Y.2d 962, 963 (1983) ("It is not unlawful to eavesdrop on telephone conversations with the consent of one of the parties to the conversation....").

But you can trust *your* claims adjuster, right? Not so fast. Remember, your insurance company doesn't want to pay the other side if the accident was your fault. This means even if you believe you're to blame, your insurance company might not be so quick to agree, which can cause real tension if you get sued, considering your policy's "duty to cooperate." This means if you believe an accident is your fault, but your insurance company doesn't want to pay the victim, you need to cooperate with your insurer.

One of the benefits of your insurance policy is that your insurance company pays for your lawyer if you get sued. Importantly, in addition to your lawyer representing you, they also represent your insurance company. This is referred to as a tripartite relationship, meaning your attorney owes a duty of loyalty to you *and* your insurer. Still, your lawyer's primary duty of loyalty is to you.

But remember who's paying your lawyer—your insurance company! Naturally, this creates a conflict because, though your lawyer has an ethical obligation to put you first, your lawyer won't want to take a position at odds with the insurer who's paying them.

For example, if you want your lawyer to admit you were at fault for an accident (meaning your insurance company would be on the hook for damages), your insurance company might not want your lawyer to—hence, your lawyer is conflicted. We're not going to work out this age-old dilemma here, but I wanted to flag it as something to have squarely in mind should this uncomfortable situation arise.

So that's the aftermath of a car crash from 30,000 feet. Now, let's get more granular and discuss some of the very specific behaviors and consequences that an auto accident invokes.

An auto accident takes only a second, but it can change your life forever. It can take years to put the pieces back together, at least as well as possible—all while not knowing whom to trust or whether you can trust anyone.

You'll have questions and plenty of them, shaped by whether the accident was your fault and the degree of your (and other people's) injuries. How should you best preserve the accident scene? How do you get your car fixed? How do you get to work in the meantime? What do you do about a rental car? Who pays for it and for how long? Do you make a claim with your insurance company or the other driver's? And if it's the other driver's, how do you do it? Do you talk to the other driver about their injuries? Do you describe your injuries to the other driver? If you think the accident was your fault, should you apologize to the other driver? How long does it take for soft tissue (non-fracture) injuries to emerge? Should you go to the emergency room? What if you don't think you were hurt?

You could always go it alone, handling the claims adjusters, police, EMS and other medical professionals, towing company, impound lot, potential civil claims, and traffic court. But I think you'd agree that's probably not the best approach. Your cost-effective alternative is, of course, to hire a lawyer.

I say "cost-effective" for a very specific reason that applies when an accident is *not* your fault. (Remember, when an accident *is* your fault, your insurance policy pays for an often-conflicted lawyer to defend you.) I'm sure you've seen billboards, sides of buses, and TV commercials advertising personal injury lawyers' services as requiring "No fee unless you win!" This is what's called a contingency fee arrangement. It means your lawyer's fee is contingent upon their winning your case. So, too, is the reimbursement of litigation expenses, such as filing fees (for filing your case in court), depositions (transcribed testimony from witnesses), and experts (specialists to help prove your case). Depending on the complexity and scale of a lawsuit, expenses can reach $100,000 or more.

The reason all states' ethical rules allow contingency fee arrangements between lawyers and clients is that without such arrangements, injury victims would rarely be able to obtain justice against wrongdoers insured by well-heeled insurers who think nothing of spending $400 or more an hour on their lawyers. In a contingency arrangement, your lawyer is your partner—you share stakes in that they only do well if they do well for you. Of all the people in this process I've listed, your lawyer is the only person you should trust.

So if you believe an auto accident wasn't your fault and you'd like to hire a lawyer, what do you get for the typical one-third to 40 percent of your case recovery that your lawyer will charge? (And all states' attorney ethical rules require the retainer agreement with your lawyer to be in writing and approved or signed by you.) You get several things:

1. Someone with experience in similar cases. Personal injury attorneys handle cases like yours daily, so they can assess your case for liability (fault) and damages and tell you whether it's worth pursuing.

2. Your personal injury attorney can sort through the facts and law required to properly pursue your case, thus allowing you to get on with your life.
3. Good personal injury attorneys employ investigators with experience in specialized areas—such as accident reconstruction, conducting witness interviews, working with claims adjusters, and gathering and reviewing medical records—who will dig into various aspects of your case.
4. Lawyers are apt to say there are three sides to every story: yours, theirs, and the truth. Your personal injury lawyer is skilled at sifting through your pain, anger, fear, and frustration to determine, as best as possible, what happened. And if they decide *you* were actually at fault, it's crucial for you to know this upfront, so you'll not only avoid disappointment but also can arrange a proper defense.
5. During the fact-finding part of your case (called discovery), the parties exchange facts and documents. The discovery process is highly technical, and your personal injury attorney knows what to provide to the other side and what to request.
6. Working with insurance companies is second nature to experienced personal injury attorneys. Insurance company tactics don't confuse or pressure them, including those that insurers use to force a quick, cheap settlement (or monetary resolution).
7. If your personal injury case is headed toward resolution short of trial, your attorney will negotiate the best possible settlement for you.

8. If your personal injury case goes to trial, your attorney will develop a legal strategy designed to get you the most compensation they can.

People also often wonder whether their insurance rates will increase after they're involved in an auto accident. That depends on who's determined to be at fault. If you were at fault, your rates will likely increase when your policy renews. But you can perhaps avoid this rate increase if your insurer offers "accident forgiveness." Insurance companies define and apply accident forgiveness differently.

For example, one insurance company might use accident forgiveness as a reward for good driving by applying a discount to your policy, while another could waive a rate increase for your first accident. Not all insurers offer accident forgiveness, so be sure to ask.

Also, eighteen states are "no-fault" states. This means they require no-fault insurance coverage, also referred to as personal injury protection insurance or PIP. This type of insurance helps cover your medical expenses and lost income if you're involved in a covered accident, regardless of who was at fault. You needn't sue the at-fault driver; instead, you file a claim with your own insurance company, which will provide benefits up to your policy limits. Because no-fault coverage involves some limitations, you might still be able to sue the at-fault driver for damages exceeding your PIP limits or for serious injuries.

Whether you hire an attorney (because an accident wasn't your fault) or your insurance company hires one for you (because the accident was), here are my top ten tips for what to do in the immediate aftermath of your accident—tips that will make things easier for your lawyer:

1. **Secure the scene:** If the vehicles are causing a safety hazard and can be moved safely, do it—for your sake and the sake of the police and EMS personnel. Several states' laws allow you to do this.
2. **Exchange information:** Be sure to get the other driver's license and insurance information. The easiest thing to do is take a picture of their license and insurance card (front and back) with your phone. Be sure to also get their phone number, as this won't be listed on these documents. Relatedly, never take a cash offer on the spot. Not only will this amount likely be less than you deserve, but it won't come with the appropriate release, meaning this short payment will only cause you legal headaches later on.
3. **Call the police:** Tell the investigating officer your side of the story and don't guess or speculate about the facts. Afterward, get a copy of the police report. Often, this requires going to the police station, but it's worth it, as what's reflected in the report could help determine whether to make a personal injury claim.
4. **Gather evidence at the crash scene:** Take photos of vehicle damage, the scene (including any skid marks, other property damage, lane configuration, and traffic signals), and any visible injuries. If the accident involved a stoplight, film an entire sequence from your point of view. This means if you had a green arrow, film the light all the way from when your green arrow illuminates to when it illuminates again.

Also, talk to witnesses and get their names and contact information. Write down or voice record the accident details while they're fresh in your mind and theirs.

Finally, keep any items that were damaged in the crash, as you could have a claim for those too.

5. **Seek medical attention:** Even if you're not in pain or think you're not injured, visit a doctor—ideally, the emergency room. Soft-tissue injuries can take a couple of days to emerge. Only a doctor can properly evaluate you and determine whether you sustained any injuries.
6. **Follow all medical advice and stick to any treatment:** Disregarding your doctor's advice or blowing off your treatment, especially physical therapy, can compromise your case and your health. Neglecting medical advice and treatment will make it appear that you weren't injured or that you don't take your injury seriously. Because if *you* don't take your injury seriously, why should the other driver's claims adjustor or the jury?
7. **Keep all documents related to your car crash:** No one cares more about your accident and obtaining the justice you deserve than you do. This means you need to keep tabs on all the documents relating to your crash. This includes medical bills, proof of lost wages, car repair invoices, etc.

   But nothing says you need to hoard paper. If you're paperless, and you'd like to scan and save everything, go for it. Just make sure everything's organized in subfolders on your hard drive or, better yet, cloud server and your email program is backed up. Because if you end up filing a lawsuit, you'll need these materials to prove your damages, meaning the amount of money you could receive for your injuries.

Relatedly, you should keep a journal of the accident, writing down the way the accident physically and mentally impacted your life. Sometimes, the possibility of a loss of consortium claim exists. That's a claim by your spouse for loss or impairment of the intangible benefits of your relationship. (In most states, loss of consortium damages are only recoverable by a spouse.) For that reason, it would be a good idea to have your spouse keep a journal, too.

8. **Stay off social media:** Everything online is "discoverable." That means not only can people see it, but also your opponent in a lawsuit can subpoena the social media platforms for your content and use it against you in your lawsuit. So let's say you're claiming a back injury from a car crash. If your Facebook feed shows you washing your car three days post-accident, and your opponent gets their hands on this data, you can imagine the cross-examination, never mind that you were in pain the entire time.

   What's more, the defense lawyer is sure to misconstrue and twist things you post online, making even benign posts look bad, such as posts about doing something with a friend or just being active and trying to live through your injury.

So save yourself these headaches and shut down your social media. It won't be forever—just as long as your lawsuit is pending.

9. **Don't talk to the other driver's insurance company or lawyers:** These people are trying to screw you—period. Nothing you say to them will help your case; it will only hurt you. If anyone talks to these people, it should be your lawyer.
10. **Hire a lawyer:** Though all of the steps are important, it's critical that you hire an experienced personal injury attorney. Often, a good lawyer is one of the most important factors contributing to a successful outcome in your personal injury case.

(And here's a super tip: Take a picture of this list with your cell phone, so you have it with you when you need it.)

I don't know about you, but my Facebook feed is crawling with faux-testimonial ads claiming I can make a mint off my car crash case without having to hire a lawyer. You know the ones: a young and attractive man or woman (apparently, someone the scam's audience can relate to) holds up a personal—*not business*—check, folded in half to cloak the payor's name and address, and insists some shadowy website immediately got them this settlement check without involving an attorney. Of course, they say you, too, can get rich if you just follow their lead.

This entire pitch reeks of too good to be true, and we all know what that means. One time, I screenshotted an actor's check and zoomed in. The check was totally fake! Another time, I clicked through one of these scams, and when I raised too many questions (and said I was going to report the firm to the state ethics board), some hack attorney called me back and berated me for meddling in his business. I kid you not!

Being the victim in a personal injury lawsuit is neither a privilege nor a money-making scheme. When you see those billboards on the highway showing someone from the waist up, crowing, "My attorney got me $2,000,000," the bottom half of this person is probably in a wheelchair. Don't fall for get-rich-quick scams or schemes and don't consider being an injury victim as an opportunity. Stay safe, and when you're hurt, protect yourself the right way.

Chapter 8
Keeping your auto insurer honest

It's bad enough to be in an auto accident, but it's even worse when your insurer denies coverage. You heard me: The auto insurer to whom you've devotedly paid premiums decides *not* to cover your accident. This can result in hundreds of thousands of dollars of exposure, potentially causing personal bankruptcy.

Here's how it happens: You make a claim with your insurance company following an accident, and for one reason or another, your insurance company sends you a coverage-denial letter, explaining in a few short sentences that your policy doesn't cover your claim. This means you're self-pay, including for your lawyers, if you're sued.

If you're wondering how this feels and how you can protect yourself, just ask me. Recently, my auto insurer denied me coverage for an auto accident involving my wife. I did the quick math, and the damages for which we could have been personally liable easily eclipsed $250,000. Needless to say, I freaked out.

Had I wanted to hire a lawyer, I'd surely have been out of luck. I wasn't seeking a pot of money from which a lawyer could take a percentage, as in a personal injury setting. I was seeking insurance coverage, and a lawyer can't take one-third of *that*. Plus, insurance companies are so obstinate that paying a lawyer by the hour would break my bank. The only option was to handle this problem myself.

Insurance policies are dense and complicated, but they're not impossible to read. In addition to a policy analysis, I needed to reconstruct a compelling story that would pay little regard to the law and complete regard to fairness. So with that foreboding windup, here's what happened and how I handled it.

In 2021, I leased a 2021 Alfa Romeo in Cleveland, Ohio, which was where we lived at the time. (I say *I* leased this car because the lease was entirely in my name—a fact that will become important.) Acme Insurance (as I'll call them) insured this vehicle, and my wife and I were listed on the insurance policy. As our two-year lease was approaching expiration, I called my friend at the dealership and asked if he had a new Alfa for us to lease after we turned in our 2021 model. He said he did, and we should swing by.

Two days before we visited the dealer, I called my Acme agent and told him we were about to switch cars. I called because we didn't want to drive even one second without auto insurance. We all know what happens then. It's the umbrella principle—it always rains when you don't have one!

He told me he would bind coverage as he'd done in the past with respect to other coverages. (Indeed, we continued receiving and paying monthly Acme bills following my phone call.) Two days later, and only after receiving my agent's assurance that he would follow my explicit instruction to ensure seamless coverage, I visited the Alfa Romeo dealer and swapped my 2021 Alfa

Romeo for a new 2024 Alfa Romeo. With complete confidence of coverage, I drove it home.

Fast forward six months. My wife was driving the 2024 Alfa in Boca Raton, Florida, when she was nailed at an intersection. Both cars were totaled, but thank goodness, nobody was badly hurt. But when I opened my Acme app to file a claim, to my dismay, I saw a reference only to the policy covering the 2021 Alfa Romeo.

What the heck could have happened? We'd been driving the 2024 car for six months, and I had instructed my agent to write coverage for it. We'd even continued to receive and pay auto insurance bills—payments Acme was all too eager to accept. When I was finally able to speak with an agent in claims, she told me, "I'm sorry, but you have no insurance on the 2024 car; you only have it on the 2021 car."

Immediately, I saw how this was going. Acme would deny coverage even though we'd instructed them to cover our new car. Sure enough, a few days later, we received a letter from Acme denying coverage on the alleged basis that we had no insurance policy on our 2024 Alfa.

This is where I freaked out. (Ask my wife.) We owed $45,000 on the car. And what if she were found to be at fault, which she wasn't, and the other car's passenger and driver were injured? They didn't seem to be, but as we've learned, soft tissue injuries can take a couple of days to emerge. Considering the other car was an Audi, the quick math added up to about $250,000 that we could owe ourselves—this, after being loyal Acme customers for over thirty years!

Because I knew this was an issue involving the policy covering my 2021 Alfa—and because Acme's coverage denial letter referred to the section of that policy defining "Insured," the first thing I did was to read my policy. (I reviewed my policy when I purchased it, and you should review yours, too, much as you don't want to.) When I read it, I couldn't believe what I saw. Just because the insurance company had told me something didn't mean it was true. Heck, that's the point of this chapter!

Under my 2021 policy, I noticed Acme defined *Insured* as someone who was in an accident while (1) driving a car owned or leased exclusively by someone else who (2) lived in their household. Hmmm, I thought—let's break down that definition.

First, was the 2021 Alfa owned or leased exclusively by someone other than my wife? Yes. It was leased exclusively by *me*. (Remember, I said we'd get to this point in a bit?) To prove this, I gathered the lease agreement, which listed only me; the loan document to the lender, which listed only me; the vehicle registration, which listed only me; and even the odometer disclosure statement, which—you guessed it—listed only me. By every measure, the car was leased by someone other than my wife. It was leased by me.

Second, I live in the same household as my wife, and I have for thirty-three years. Alongside the previous point, the easy-to-obtain facts demonstrated that my wife *was* an insured on our 2021 policy for the accident involving our 2024 vehicle. Put another way, coverage on the 2024 vehicle wasn't predicated on our having an insurance policy for that car. According to Acme's own policy language, we had coverage for that vehicle through the policy on our 2021 vehicle.

That was the easy argument. But because I believe in a belt-and-suspenders approach, I was intent on leveraging the fact that our Acme agent failed to place coverage on the 2024 vehicle—meaning he failed to write us a new policy—which resulted in the foregoing machinations. Wouldn't it also help if Acme were barred—or "estopped"—from denying coverage because we had relied on Acme only for it to screw us over? Of course, it would.

That was my next argument, and it required climbing atop my forensic horse and really unpacking the facts, which I knew would be a long, tough slog involving cell phone records, emails, letters, and policy documents. But with a quarter of a million dollars potentially at stake, believe me, I had little better to do.

I remembered calling my agent's office and talking to his assistant only days before trading in my 2021 vehicle for the 2024 vehicle. So I jumped on T-Mobile's website to see whether my cell phone call log reflected any calls to or from my agent in the days preceding my visit to the dealer.

I keyed in the month I visited the dealer, held my breath, and pressed *Enter*. To my delight, three Acme-related calls lit up my screen—two from me to the agency, followed by one from the agency to me. I focused on the second and third calls, which occurred on the Thursday before I visited the Alfa dealer. My fact-finding mission was off to a great start.

The second call was a short one from me to the agency. This was when I left a voicemail for a return call. The third was a longer call from my agency to me shortly afterward. That was when I advised Acme of our lease swap and instructed them to bind coverage to the 2024 Alfa Romeo.

Unfortunately, the agency didn't record calls—our agent's assistant told me that. What if the agent admitted to the conversation but denied it was related to the new coverage? Anticipating this defense, I continued my investigation, now searching for evidence ruling out anything *other than* my instruction to swap auto coverage.

I took to my emails to see whether I'd had any other conversations with our insurance agent around that time. Three insurance-related issues emerged, but I was able to rule them out. The first concerned a business policy my wife wanted our agent to place for her new company.

Remember, how I said I saw *three* phone calls in the T-Mobile log? Here's where the first call comes in. I found an email from me to my wife that followed this first call by just a few minutes. In my email, I told her how I had just instructed our agent to place a business policy for her.

So not only could the second and third calls, which occurred only two days before our lease swap, *not* have involved my wife's business coverage (because that issue was resolved following the first call that occurred three weeks *before* the second and third calls), but our agency also never ended up placing this coverage. Remember this fact because it'll become an important part of the story.

Next, my wife and I had just sold our house, and we were about to move in with my father-in-law while we transitioned. My wife emailed our agency explaining that we needed to seamlessly convert our homeowners' policy to a renters' policy. Because the declarations page of this new renters' policy was dated three days *before* the second and third calls, these calls could not have involved our renters' coverage—our agency had already placed it.

Notably, despite my wife's request, our agency actually failed to make our coverage seamless and allowed a day of uninsured time to exist between policies. You needn't be an insurance-coverage lawyer to know that had my father-in-law's house burned down that night, Acme would have denied coverage. Remember this fact, too.

Finally, around the time of the lease swap, my wife lost her watch, but we didn't make a claim on that until almost two weeks *after* the second and third calls. That meant this issue could not have been the reason for the phone calls either.

And to the extent Acme might have thought I just woke up on the morning I swapped my cars and figured, "I think I'll get a new car today," I discovered an email from myself to my friend at the Alfa dealer inquiring about swapping the cars. I sent this email five days *before* the second and third calls, meaning getting a new car was easily on my mind when I talked to my agency.

My point, of course, is that I was able to prove—not merely allege—that the only topic I discussed with my agent two days before visiting the dealer was getting seamless auto insurance coverage, no different than when we'd insisted on seamless homeowners' coverage, and a homeowners' claim is tons less likely than an auto claim.

So that was my factual story, derived from the common-sense observation that I needed to show—not tell—Acme that we'd instructed it to place coverage, and it dropped the ball. There was absolutely no law infused into that story; it involved only the facts.

In the following letter, you'll see I *did* get into the law. It's what I do. But it turns out it wasn't necessary, as I'll explain. After all, often, it's not the law that drives a decision, whether by a judge or an insurance adjuster. Instead, it's about the story, meaning it's about the facts. And I knew I had great ones. So in my letter, you'll see precisely how I told my story, and I hope you'll be able to pluck themes and turns of phrase if you ever need to go toe-to-toe with your insurer.

Where most people would simply accept the insurer's coverage denial as the final word, my letter and the preceding explanation will hopefully reorient your thinking. I'd encourage you to push back and ask commonsense questions where your rights—and money—are at stake.

So check out my letter. Yes, it's long and dense. That's because it includes several elements *you* might need to fashion a meaningful letter if *you're* ever in my incredibly scary situation.

Pay mind to how I begin by examining the policy, which is something you can read and understand, especially if you've read my letter below and don't have a victim mentality. You'll next see how I dive into the facts, which is something you should be able to do easily because you lived through them.

And if you choose not to dig into my deep treatment now, that's okay. Just know you have a robust resource if you are in a terrifying insurance-coverage dispute. Indeed, you can likely adapt my letter's concepts for use if you have a homeowners' or other coverage issue. So buckle up because, believe me, if this happened to me, it could happen to you.

RE:	Claim Number 277-614C5-19F
Date of Loss	March 3, 2024
Insured	Daniel R. Karon
Place of Incident	SW 18th St. & Via De Sonrisa Del Norte, Boca Raton, FL
Policy Number	259482367-2303-5

Dear Sir or Madam,

This letter is in response to Acme's March 5, 2023, coverage denial letter, Exhibit A, wherein Acme denied coverage related to an automobile accident that occurred on March 3, 2024, based on an erroneous interpretation of the Karons' auto insurance policy, Exhibit B, and incomplete facts. For the following reasons, coverage exists.

A. Miriam Karon is an insured under the Karons' auto insurance policy.

According to Exhibit B, "***Insured*** means… ***you*** for the…use of a ***car owned by***…a ***person*** who resides primarily in ***your*** household. That ***car*** cannot be ***owned by you***…." Exhibit B at 4. Exhibit B next explains that "***Owned By*** means…leased, if the lease is written for a period of thirty-one or more consecutive days." *Id.* at 3. Finally, Exhibit B instructs that Acme "will pay damages if an ***insured*** becomes legally liable to pay because of…***bodily injury*** to others; and…damage to property caused by an accident that involves a vehicle for which that ***insured*** is provided Liability Coverage by this policy." *Id.* at 4.

For reasons I will describe shortly, Miriam Karon was driving the Karons' 2024—not 2021—Alfa Romeo Stelvio when her March 3, 2024, accident occurred. But Miriam was not the lessee of this 2024 Alfa Romeo Stelvio—her husband Daniel Karon was. What's more, Miriam and Daniel reside in the same household and have for over thirty years.

Additionally, Daniel's name—*not* Miriam's—is on the Motor Vehicle Lease Buyer's Order for the 2024 Alfa Romeo Stelvio, Exhibit C; Daniel's name—*not* Miriam's is on the Odometer Disclosure Statement for the 2024 Alfa Romeo Stelvio, Exhibit D; Daniel's name—*not* Miriam's—is on the lease for the 2024 Alfa Romeo Stelvio, Exhibit E; and Daniel's name—*not* Miriam's—is on the Certificate of Registration. Exhibit F. Miriam's name appears nowhere on any of the transactional documents related to the 2024 Alfa Romeo Stelvio. Accordingly, and as instructed by Exhibit B, the 2024 Alfa Romeo Stelvio is "Owned By" Daniel—*not* Miriam—Karon.

Exhibit B defines as an Insured a person (Miriam) who uses a car Owned By another person (Daniel) so long as the owner resides primarily in the same household as the Insured, which Daniel does. And to this Insured, Acme owes a duty to pay claims owed by the Insured (*not* to say Miriam owes damages) for bodily injury and property damage.

Yet Acme denied coverage, focusing not on the foregoing policy language but instead exclusively on whether Daniel's 2024 Alfa Romeo Stelvio was a "Newly Acquired Car." *See* Exhibit A. This misguided analysis ignores Acme policy language defining Miriam as an Insured for purposes of coverage for bodily injury and property damage. Perhaps Acme failed to conduct the foregoing analysis because it lacked information demonstrating that the 2024 Alfa Romeo Stelvio was leased to Daniel and that Daniel and Miriam have resided in the same household for over thirty years. But whether or not the 2024 Alfa Romeo Stelvio was newly acquired, Acme's unambiguous policy language provided Miriam coverage for bodily injury and property damage related to her March 3, 2024, accident.

Only the accident, which involves tort liability—*not* insurance coverage—occurred in Florida. According to Florida's most-significant-relationship test, Ohio law applies to our coverage question. *See Sturiano v. Brooks*, 523 So.2d 1126, 1129 (Fla. 1988) ("[A]s applied to insurance contracts,...the law of the jurisdiction where the contract was executed governs the rights and liabilities of the parties in determining an issue of insurance coverage."); Restatement (Second) of Conflict of Laws § 188(1) (1971) ("The rights and duties of the parties with respect to an issue in contract are determined by the local law of the state which, with respect to that issue, has the most significant relationship to the transaction and the parties....").

Ohio likewise adopts the most-significant-relationship test. *See Ohayon v. Safeco Ins. Co.*, 91

Ohio St.3d 474, 477 (2001) ("[I]n the absence of an effective choice of law by the parties, their rights and duties under the contract are determined by the law of the state that, with respect to that issue, has 'the most significant relationship to the transaction and the parties.'" (quoting Restatement (Second) of Conflicts at § 188(1) (1971))). Applying Ohio's conflict-of-law jurisprudence also results in the conclusion that Ohio coverage law applies.

B. Notwithstanding the preceding (and unambiguous) policy interpretation, Acme is estopped from denying the Karons' coverage for the March 3, 2024, accident, because Daniel instructed Acme to provide them seamless coverage between the 2021 Alfa Romeo Stelvio and the 2024 Alfa Romeo Stelvio, yet Acme failed to do so.

The below-described facts demonstrate that on September 28, 2023—two days *before* Daniel leased his 2024 Alfa Romeo Stelvio—he called his Acme agent Yosemite Sam. Daniel spoke to Sam's assistant Wile E. Coyote and explained he was about to lease a 2024 Alfa Romeo Stelvio.

Because Daniel is meticulous about insurance coverage, he requested Coyote ensure him in no uncertain terms that continuous coverage would exist as he transitioned from his 2021

Alfa Romeo Stelvio to the 2024 Alfa Romeo Stelvio.

Coyote ensured Daniel that continuous coverage would exist after which Daniel continued to pay his electronically received monthly auto insurance bills, expecting Coyote had done for him what he requested and Coyote promised—namely, provide seamless and continuous coverage from one vehicle to the next.

To this end, the timeline below proves several things:

- Daniel called Acme on September 28, 2023, to discuss the necessity for continuous coverage from one vehicle to the next;
- It rules out the possibility that Karon's September 28, 2023, phone calls related to matters other than continuous automobile coverage (e.g., transitioning his homeowners' coverage to renters' coverage or making a claim for a lost watch); and
- It demonstrates Acme's past neglect and inadvertence, which includes (during the less than two months depicted) two additional times where Acme, through Sam's office, failed to provide coverage the Karons requested and relied upon and that Acme promised—once for Miriam's new business and another related to the Karons' transition between their homeowners' coverage and renters' coverage. [Remember, I asked you to keep in mind that Acme had twice failed to provide us

with coverage? Here's where I exploited that fact as demonstrating a pattern of Acme's carelessness.]

Event timeline

8/24/23	Email from Coyote to Miriam regarding business insurance, attaching a quote and asking for her father's address as the Karons were about to move in with him—Exhibit G
8/24/23	Email from Miriam to Coyote providing Coyote her father's address and indicating she would review the business insurance policy Coyote sent to her—Exhibit H
8/30/23	Email from Coyote to Miriam asking when the move to her father's house would occur—Exhibit I
8/30/23	Email from Miriam to Coyote explaining that the move to her father's would occur on September 23, 2023—Exhibit J
9/6/23	Daniel's two-minute call to Coyote (3:25 p.m.)—Exhibit K

9/6/23	Daniel's email to Miriam describing his discussion with Coyote minutes earlier about her business insurance wherein he instructed Coyote to commence coverage, yet *Coyote never commenced this coverage and still hasn't* (3:57 p.m.)—Exhibit L
9/23/23	Email from Daniel to Elmer Fudd at Alfa Romeo of Looney Tunes, Ohio, inquiring about the cost of a 2024 Alfa Stelvio to replace his 2021 Alfa Stelvio—Exhibit M
9/25/23	Proof of renters' insurance commencing per renters' policy's declarations page but two days *after* 9/23/23—the date Miriam Karon instructed Coyote on 8/30/23 that renters' coverage needed to be in effect—Exhibit N
9/28/23	Daniel's two-minute call to Coyote (9:41 a.m.)—Exhibit K
9/28/23	Coyote's three-minute call to Daniel (1:33 p.m.)—Exhibit K
9/30/23	Document from Elmer Fudd showing 9/30/23 "CONTRACT START" date for 2024 Alfa Romeo Stelvio—Exhibit O

10/11/23	Miriam made claim with Coyote for her lost watch—Exhibit P
11/28/23	Email exchange between Daniel and Coyote adding his watch to personal articles policy—Exhibit Q

C. Daniel instructed Acme—and Acme promised—to provide continuous coverage as he transitioned from his 2021 Alfa Romeo Stelvio to his 2024 Alfa Romeo Stelvio.

Though Coyote claimed to Daniel during their March 4, 2024, telephone conversation that no record of calls to him or his office existed that predated by a few days the purchase of Daniel's 2024 Alfa Romeo Stelvio, Exhibit K proves otherwise. *See* Exhibit R (Affidavit of Daniel R. Karon).

As Exhibit K demonstrates, Daniel had at least one or two talks with Coyote a mere two days before he leased his 2024 Alfa Romeo Stelvio, wherein Daniel told Coyote of the need for—and Coyote promised to immediately place—coverage on the 2024 Alfa Romeo Stelvio that he was leasing two days later. *Id.* at ¶ 6. These discussions occurred on a Thursday, and Daniel leased his new car on Saturday, as Exhibit N demonstrates.

Finally, Exhibit M proves that by September 23, 2023, Daniel was contemplating leasing a 2024 Alfa Romeo Stelvio, meaning this topic did not arise only *after* his September 28, 2023, calls to and from Coyote.[2]

a. Daniel's September 28, 2023, calls to Coyote were for the exclusive purpose of ensuring continuous automobile coverage as he transitioned from his 2021 Alfa Romeo Stelvio to his 2024 Alfa Romeo Stelvio.

Two other insurance matters were underway around the time Daniel leased his 2024 Alfa Romeo Stelvio—the Karons' transition from a homeowners' policy to a renters' policy and a claim for Miriam's watch. But Daniel's September 28, 2023, calls to and conversation with Coyote cannot plausibly be ascribed to either of these other insurance-related matters.

First, the Karons' renters' policy became effective on September 25, 2023. This means any discussions concerning its scope and contours necessarily occurred *before* this policy's issue date reflected in Exhibit J. Second, Miriam didn't make her claim for her watch until October 11, 2023—almost two weeks *after* Daniel's calls to and from Coyote. *See* Exhibit P.

---

2 Daniel's exchange with Coyote concerning adjusting his automobile coverage is consistent with their practice of Daniel calling and/or emailing requests for policy adjustments. See Exhibit S.

The evidence proves that no other insurance-related needs or discussions could have given rise to Daniel's September 28, 2023, calls to and from Coyote other than Daniel's need for—and Coyote's promise to guarantee—continuous automobile coverage as Daniel transitioned from his 2021 Alfa Romeo Stelvio to his 2024 Alfa Romeo Stelvio. Indeed, the Karons have continued to pay premiums on their automobile policy (as recently as only a few days ago), with Acme all too eager to accept these payments.

b. If Acme's neglect to provide the Karons continuous coverage as Daniel transitioned from his 2021 Alfa Romeo Stelvio to his 2024 Alfa Romeo Stelvio weren't bad enough, Acme, through Coyote and Sam, have a history of neglect and inadvertence as it concerns providing coverage promised to the Karons.

This isn't the first (or even second) time Acme has failed to provide coverage it promised the Karons. Exhibit G demonstrates Miriam's interest in Coyote placing business insurance coverage for her. Exhibit L demonstrates Daniel's instruction for Coyote to place this business insurance coverage, yet *Coyote never did.*

On August 30, 2023, Miriam explained to Coyote that the move to her father's would occur on September 23, 2023, meaning it was essential that renters' coverage commence on September 23, 2023. *See* Exhibit C. Yet Coyote did not initiate the Karons' renters' coverage until September 25, 2023. *See* Exhibit N.

This means had the Karons suffered a loss on September 24, 2023 (the date during which coverage did not exist), Acme would have denied them coverage despite their instruction to Coyote to place it and Coyote's agreement to do so. *See, e.g., Tate v. U.S. Fin. Life Ins. Co.*, No. 02:04cv0820, 2006 U.S. Dist. LEXIS 62603, at *17 (W.D. Pa. Sep. 1, 2006) (granting summary judgment to insurer where "[d]ecedent did not accept the terms of the policy while he was still alive by signing the delivery documents and paying the premium.").

Also, considering the fastidiousness with which the Karons regarded their property-coverage situation—ensuring they were not uninsured for even one second—it is implausible to believe Daniel would have allowed his automobile to go uninsured for months, especially when considering the significantly higher likelihood of incurring an auto claim than a property claim.

In this manner, Acme, via Coyote, failed to provide requested-and-promised coverage *twice* before the current incident, thus evidencing Acme's pattern of neglect and inadvertence, which shortcomings can plausibly be ascribed to Acme's behavior here.

What's more, the Karons have been Acme insured for over thirty years (about twenty-five with Yosemite Sam), they hold multiple policies, they have always paid their premiums on time, they routinely refer their friends to Acme, and they have a modest claims history. But despite all this, and the Karons' vital need to talk to their agent Yosemite Sam concerning the March 3, 2023, accident, it wasn't until *March 7, 2023*, that Sam finally returned their countless excruciating phone calls, merely claiming he would "go to bat" for them yet providing no detail during their mere four-minute phone call.

While painfully awaiting Sam's call, Daniel asked Coyote why Sam refused to call them. Coyote confessed that Sam was on vacation, though Sam checked in routinely with Coyote and knew all about the Karons' situation yet refused to call them.

c. Because of Coyote's false promises upon which Daniel relied and from which serious consequences have arisen, Acme is estopped from denying coverage to the Karons for the March 3, 2024, accident.

To prevail on a claim for promissory estoppel, plaintiff must demonstrate "[a] promise which the promisor should reasonably expect to induce action or forbearance on the part of the promisee or a third person and which does induce such action or forbearance is binding if injustice can be avoided only by enforcement of the promise." *Mers v. Dispatch Printing Co.*, 19 Ohio St.3d 100, 483 N.E.2d 150 (1985).

Via Coyote on September 28, 2023, Acme promised Daniel continuous coverage on his 2024 Alfa Romeo Stelvio no differently than the way Coyote promised Miriam business insurance coverage via the Karons' telephonic and email exchanges with him and renters' coverage commencing on September 23, 2023, via Coyote's email exchanges with Miriam.

On account of Coyote's interactions with Daniel related to Daniel's need for continuous automobile coverage (along with Coyote's knowledge of Daniel's diligence to insurance matters—e.g., the renters' insurance situation), Coyote would have reasonably expected his promise concerning continuous automobile coverage to induce Daniel to believe he was providing such coverage such that Daniel would forbear from obtaining other coverage.

And Coyote's promise, in fact, induced Daniel to rely on it such that Daniel understood and proceeded on his understanding that Coyote's promised coverage existed. Daniel forbore obtaining coverage for his 2024 Alfa Romeo Stelvio as he reasonably understood it was unnecessary because of the coverage Coyote promised on September 28, 2023, to provide him for his swapped vehicle. *See* Exhibit R at ¶ 11.

Finally, injustice can be avoided only by enforcement of the promise Coyote made because without coverage Daniel will be responsible for considerable costs after seamlessly paying for coverage following possession of his 2024 Alfa Romeo Stelvio.

D. Conclusion

The facts and law lead to but one conclusion—Acme owes the Karons coverage for the March 3, 2024, accident. If Acme maintains its refusal to provide coverage, the Karons will file suit in federal court, alleging bad faith and seeking attorneys' fees. They will also consider the possibility of a federal class-action lawsuit on behalf of other Acme policyholders to whom Acme has denied coverage under similar circumstances.

I look forward to receiving Acme's notice reversing its coverage decision.

Very truly yours,
s/Daniel R. Karon
Daniel R. Karon

This letter was a *tour de force* but for good reason. Law school-level treatment. That's because I was looking at having to pay a quarter of a million dollars if I didn't do what was required to fix the situation. Wouldn't you agree that level of risk required pulling out all the stops?

I'm pleased to share that about two weeks after I sent my letter, I received a call from a claims adjuster, apologizing for how Acme had treated us. And though I thought the contract-interpretation argument was the stronger argument, which is why I led with it, the claims adjuster didn't say a word about it. Instead, she focused exclusively on my story and the unjustness Acme had forced upon us.

In the end, not only did Acme agree to cover everything related to the accident, but it even reimbursed us for a car payment we made while this whole mess played out.

I genuinely hope you never end up in the crosshairs of your insurance company like we did. But if you do, I also hope you'll see that perhaps there is a way to get out of them, depending on your facts, and that you might not need to be a lawyer to do it.

Adapt the elements of my letter to your situation. It's because of the unlikelihood that you'll find a lawyer who's willing to help that I presented the ultradeep dive I did for you here.

Because take it from me, if you don't advocate for yourself, nobody will. But now that you know not only that you can push back but also, via my letter, *how* you can push back, defend yourself, and don't let anyone (especially an insurance company) tell you the score. And though I can't guarantee positive results, I *can* tell you that doing nothing guarantees only one result, and it most certainly won't be a good one.

Chapter 9
Understanding ugly liability waivers (because they're everywhere)

I once wondered if, when buying a ticket to a music festival, I was signing away my right to make a claim if something happened to me that was the festival's fault, such as the merchandise tent collapsed on me or the porta-potty tipped over while I was inside. (Gross, I know, but you-know-what happens!)

There was no language on the ticket limiting the festival's liability, but that didn't provide me peace of mind. So I looked more closely at the electronic ticket I'd already bought and paid for and noticed something else. Discreetly tucked at the bottom were the words "Terms and Conditions."

Always a red flag.

I clicked on this language. But, again, there was no reference to anything alarming. Except, wait—there was another link. When I clicked *that* link, I found what I was looking for in a place where nobody was likely to see it, much less before they purchased their ticket.

It said I waived my right to pursue a claim relating to the music festival's negligence, as if simply saying this made it true. This language is what the law calls a "liability waiver"—a document that protects businesses from lawsuits. Liability waivers are everywhere, and believe me, they don't help you. Instead, they can make a very bad situation, such as an accident, much worse by giving the company that hurt you a legal basis for evading responsibility, thus potentially leaving you to pay for your medical bills and other damages.

These days, everyone is so interested in covering their rear end that it's difficult to do anything or go anywhere without having to sign an ugly (and often secret) liability waiver. These risk-mitigation tools are usually hidden as I just described. They're on the back of a paper contract, receipt, or invoice or buried deep in a website that requires several drags and clicks to possibly see it.

This language generally proposes one of two uninviting things: The company is free from liability arising from its negligence or wrongdoing regarding a particular activity, or the company is free from liability arising out of the performance of the contract, whose language is much broader than the first option. Both versions purport to excuse the company from any liability resulting from loss or damage you sustain due to the company's carelessness.

Often, the terms "liability waiver" and "release of liability" are used interchangeably. I gave my music festival example to demonstrate how companies routinely bury this language in their contracts and websites. But let's knock out a few more common examples structured to screw you that you might not have considered. Though you've likely seen the following language (or perhaps you haven't), now you'll understand its effect:

- You leave your car with a valet, who drives it off. Problem is, he never drives it back because he totaled it on the way to the parking lot. Turns out, he was texting while driving. That's why he crashed. But your claim ticket contains "release of liability" language excusing the valet company from damages resulting from its negligence. So when you make a claim for your car, they tell you, "Tough luck."

- You join a health club because it's time to get in shape. You sign up online, dragging and clicking through a series of webpages, affixing your electronic signature where required, never noticing that buried in the lengthy terms and conditions is a "liability waiver."

  One day in the locker room, a locker door falls on your head. Turns out, the maintenance staff forgot to replace the screws in the hinges when fixing it. Because this resulted in a concussion, you want to make a claim for your damages, which includes lost wages. But the club responds that its liability waiver exempts it from liability related to its negligence.

- You take a load of clothes to the dry cleaner, including your favorite sweater. They tell you to come back on Tuesday. But when you do, everything's ready except the sweater.

  The dry cleaner is at a loss to explain where it is and asks you to come back the next day. When you do, the

> sweater is still missing. When you tell the dry cleaner you'd like to recoup the cost of the sweater, they invite you to review your receipt, which, you guessed it, contains a release of liability.

But liability waivers and releases from liability don't hide only in your contracts. They hide in plain sight. Think about warning signs posted on playgrounds, at sports arenas, construction sites, or other places where you could end up getting hurt. Often, the language is subtle, such as, "Use of playground equipment is at your own risk," "Park at your own risk," "Enter at your own risk," or "Not responsible for damaged property." What the people in charge of these properties are really saying is, "We were completely negligent when we forgot to secure the legs of a swing to the ground, but no matter; if the swing collapses and hurts your kid, you can't sue us."

Liability waivers and releases also routinely "appear" in software download licenses. These agreements are the fine print you see but likely ignore when you click or scroll through the Terms and Conditions necessary for accessing pretty much any online service.

Simply put, a waiver or release is a contract that customers sign with vendors before a service or activity commences. By signing (or clicking), customers agree, in advance, to excuse the vendor from any and all liability for injuries resulting from the vendor's negligence. In this manner, vendors are relieved from exercising ordinary care to keep their customers safe.

A typical waiver of liability form related to participating in a physical activity looks like the following, but all waivers and releases are conceptually the same. Look at the dangerous language buried in this clickwrap agreement:

Section 6. Releases:

In exchange for You being allowed to use any of the Services, Ultra Bike bicycles, Stations, Bike Docks, or related information, You...do hereby fully and forever release and discharge all Released Persons for all Claims that You have or may have against any Released Person, except for Claims caused by the Released Person's gross negligence or willful misconduct. Such releases are intended to be general and complete releases of all Claims. The Released Persons may plead such releases as a complete and sufficient defense to any Claim, as intended 3rd beneficiaries of such releases.

The Release Agreement defines "claims" as "any and all claims, injuries, demands, liabilities, disputes, causes of action (including statutory, contract, negligence, or other tort theories), proceedings [or] damages that arise from or relate to (a) any of the Services, including any of the Ultra Bike bicycles, Stations, Bike Docks, or related information...." "Released Persons" is defined in the Agreement, as relevant, as including: "(i) NY123 and all of its owners, managers, affiliates, employees, agents, representatives, successors, and assigns, [and] (ii) the City of New York."

Section 7. Disclaimers:

You do hereby acknowledge and agree that your use of any of the services, Ultra Bike bicycles, stations, bike docks, or related information, is at your sole risk.... All of the services, Ultra Bike bicycles, stations, bike docks, or related information are provided "as is" and "as available" (and you rely on them solely at your own risk).... You assume full responsibility and risk of loss for using any of the services, Ultra Bike bicycles, stations, bike docks, or related information, and NY123 and all other released persons are not liable for any claim attributable to any of the foregoing.

Section 8. Limited Liability:

You do hereby acknowledge and agree that, except as may otherwise be limited by New York General Obligation Law Section 5-326, NY123 and all other released persons are not responsible or liable for any claim, including those that arise out of or relate to (A) any risk, danger or hazard described in the Agreement, (B) Your use of or inability to use, any of the services, Ultra Bike bicycles, stations, bike docks, or related information, (C) your breach of this agreement or your violation of any law, (D) any negligence, misconduct, or other action or inaction by you, (E) your failure to wear a bicycle helmet while using Ultra Bike

> bicycle, or (F) any negligence, misconduct, or other action or inaction of any third party. You do hereby waive all claims with respect to any of the foregoing, including those based in contract, tort (including negligence), statutory, or other grounds, even if NY123 or any of the other released persons has been advised of the possibility of such claims. The total liability of NY123 and all other released persons for all claims, including those based in contract, tort (including negligence), statutory, or other grounds, is limited to the sum of $100.
>
> Section 9. Assumption of Risk by Member:
>
> Member agrees that riding an Ultra Bike bicycle involves many obvious and not-so-obvious risks, dangers, and hazards, which may result in injury or death to Member or others, as well as damage to property, and that such risks, dangers, and hazards cannot always be predicted or avoided. Member agrees that such risks, dangers, and hazards are Member's sole responsibility.

(By the way, and related to this topic by virtue of its sleaziness, a website I visited to find typical release language required me to buy a seven-day subscription for $1.95. No big deal. But snuck into the subscription process was the following language: "You'll be charged $1.95 ($1.95 subtotal, $0.00 tax) for your seven-day trial. Your trial ends on 7/11/2024. If you don't cancel your trial by that date, we'll charge you $37.00 plus applicable taxes per month until you cancel your plan. Charges won't be refunded unless they are legally required. All amounts shown are in USD." This is called a "negative option," which is a business practice whereby customers are given goods or services they didn't previously order and must continue to pay for the service—or specifically decline it—before billing. Negative options are something to watch for because they're almost as ubiquitous as liability waivers and releases.)

Did you see that each paragraph in Ultra Bike's release involved a different kind of liability waiver? That's because liability waivers come in several shapes and sizes that you need to recognize because they could (and are designed to) affect your health and wallet.

Here are some other types of waivers and releases to watch for:

> **Shrink-wrap and clickwrap agreements.** Liability waivers and releases are often hidden in shrink-wrap and clickwrap agreements. (Ultra Bike's was a clickwrap agreement.) These "agreements" are the fine print you "see" when you click through terms and conditions related to making online purchases from product retailers or when agreeing to online licensing, often involving software downloads.
>
> The term "shrink-wrap" derives from the manufacturing process of shrinking clear cellophane packaging around a product box. Often, the document with the anticonsumer language was packaged in the box, meaning the consumer couldn't see it till after the purchase.

Clickwrap agreements are a more sinister form of shrink-wrap agreements in that they are designed to encourage your assent. They require you to click through various pages of small print, physically "agreeing" to every page along the way. Big business claims this process allows the parties to facilitate contracting, but the real reason is to enable the company to argue that you overtly agreed to its terms as opposed to having simply missed them.

Whether your shrink-wrap or clickwrap agreement is for a product or service, you can bet it will include non-negotiable terms and conditions, such as the anti-consumer language contained in Ultra Bike's agreement and those described below.

Preinjury releases. A preinjury release or waiver resembles the waiver and release quoted above, except it's a bit narrower. It's a document customers sign before an event that excuses the vendors from injuries resulting from the vendor's negligence.

A typical preinjury release reads like this:

> Release of Liability. I hereby release and discharge Crazy Skydiving and all other Releasees from any and all liability, claims, demands, or causes of action that I may hereafter have for INJURY, DEATH or DAMAGES arising out of my participation in Skydiving Activities even if caused by negligence or other fault of Crazy Skydiving or any other

> Releasee or the skydiving operator engaged by Crazy Skydiving.

What courts consider to be an enforceable release varies from state to state. Some states strictly construe waivers and releases, while others are more forgiving and consider whether consumers had fair notice of the waiver and release, a "meeting of the minds" existed, and consumers received something in exchange for giving up their rights—a legal concept known as *consideration.*

Indemnification and hold-harmless agreements. Indemnification and hold-harmless agreements are similar to waivers and releases but not identical. The main difference is that hold-harmless agreements require consumers to protect vendors against actual *and potential* losses, while indemnification agreements require consumers to protect vendors against actual losses, though several states consider these agreements synonymous.

Put another way, indemnity is an offensive right, meaning vendors must seek it against customers for money that vendors have spent related to their negligence, while hold-harmless agreements create a defensive right where vendors tell customers, "Don't bother me." Similar to each other and similarly nasty.

Covenants not to sue. A covenant not to sue is a legal agreement that prevents customers from suing vendors relating to a dispute arising from their relationship, whether based on negligence, breach of contract, or whatever.

But a covenant not to sue differs from the waivers and releases we've been discussing. Remember, a release of liability is a waiver of a known right, but a covenant not to sue isn't. A covenant not to sue preserves the claim while limiting your right to file a lawsuit. Different approach, same result—you're left holding the bag.

Disclaimers. Disclaimers purport to limit a vendor's risk. A common disclaimer is "Enter at your own risk." Also popular are "Use at your own risk," "Wet floor," "Not responsible for loss or damage to your vehicle," and "Back off." (I see a lot of the last one on semi trucks' mudflaps below an image of Yosemite Sam [not my insurance agent], wielding two six-shooters.) And, of course, there's the ubiquitous "Beware of Dog."

Though a disclaimer might put customers on notice of a dangerous condition, it doesn't let vendors off the hook. At best, a court might hold an injured customer "contributorily liable" for their injury, meaning they're partially at fault for having "assumed the risk."

So does this mean you can't drive behind a semi because the driver told you not to via their mudflaps? Of course not. If there were an accident, the driver could be responsible for your injuries so long as a jury found you less than fifty (or in some states fifty-one) percent at fault.

And another word on "Beware of Dog." That disclaimer might actually work *against* the pet owner, as it admits their dog is dangerous and susceptible to causing injury. Where a dog owner is on notice that their

> dog is dangerous, this knowledge can change an injury case alleging simple negligence into a claim alleging wantonness that supports punitive damages.

Those are the most common means by which big businesses try to screw you. Betcha didn't know there was so much they were trying to get away with.

And don't think companies didn't slip in liability waivers during COVID. Remember when your kid couldn't attend soccer practice or you couldn't get a haircut unless you signed one? In like manner, liability waivers are often tucked into boxes containing new cell phones or other products, meaning you necessarily couldn't have agreed to them as part of your purchase.

Finally, and to make matters even worse, liability waivers and releases often dwell in "adhesion contracts" (take-it-or-leave-it contracts), which are agreements that contain non-negotiable terms and conditions. Think of cell phone providers' contracts; even if you don't like the terms in one, you will see them in all the others. And good luck striking language from your cell phone contract and having the store manager sign off on it. This means you have no choice but to accept the adhesion contract to obtain the product or service.

Taken together, what does this mean for us? Was this long discussion merely to educate you about what you sign and click? If so, though you're informed, you probably feel pretty helpless—perhaps to the point where you wish I hadn't shared this with you.

But don't despair. Many judges know that regular people never see—much less read—liability waivers, especially when hidden, as with my music festival waiver. And even if people did read them, granting companies a get-out-of-jail-free card for their negligence is often a bridge too far because liability waivers, often buried in dense legal documents, are so ugly and anticonsumer that some courts refuse to enforce them as written, if at all.

Though much of the law these days tends to favor big business, the law still strives to channel our societal norms and mores. Courts do their best to balance consumers' rights to recover damages for another's negligence with the ability of businesses to conduct activities that involve risk without being subjected to lawsuits every time somebody is hurt or property is lost or damaged. To this end, some courts will invalidate liability waivers and releases they believe are overreach or unreasonable, whether liability waivers, releases, assumption-of-risk agreements, liability disclaimers, sign postings, or whatever.

Courts channel their refusals to enforce through the legal doctrine of "unconscionability," which is a fancy way of saying "unfairness." Unconscionability splits into two tracks that courts balance: "procedural" unconscionability and "substantive" unconscionability.

Procedural unconscionability considers how the waiver language appears in the contract or agreement. Where it's at the bottom, on the last screen where you need to click half a dozen times, appears only by cross reference, is in three-point or lighter-color font as compared to the rest of the text, or is inside the box only to be discovered after your purchase, many (but not all) courts will consider the waiver too unfair to be enforceable. (That said, some courts see no problem with these techniques.) This could be an important ruling if, for instance, a vendor is trying to wriggle out of a negligence claim for its product having hurt you or a contract claim for its product having cost you business losses.

Substantive unconscionability examines the egregiousness of the waiver's language and whether it's simply too nasty to be enforced. So where a waiver is relatively conspicuous but especially ugly—for instance, it exempts the vendor from any liability relating to its negligence, even if gross (meaning a reckless disregard for the rights and welfare of others) or extreme—a court might refuse to enforce the language based on a high level of substantive unconscionability and modest level of procedural unconscionability.

See how the balancing works? Courts tend to consider unconscionability—and an agreement's concomitant enforceability—on a sliding scale: Where there's a lot of substantive unconscionability, less procedural unconscionability is required for a court to declare a liability waiver and release invalid and vice versa. Notably, the way courts treat unconscionability and the enforceability of liability waivers and releases often depends on the law of the state where the drafter is attempting to enforce them.

So that's a bit on the law concerning waivers and releases. Now, as we do in law school, how about we channel some actual facts through the law to see how waiver-and-release law affects people in real life? Remember that bike-share release I described earlier? Let's use that case—this time with real names for authenticity.

Corwin v. NYC Bike Share, LLC, 238 F. Supp. 3d 475 (S.D.N.Y. 2017), involved a bicycle accident suffered by Ronald Corwin, an annual member of New York City's Citi Bike bicycle-rental program. He was riding the New York City streets without a helmet (never a good idea) when he collided with a concrete wheel stop, violently striking his head and suffering serious injury on the cement.

Though Corwin sued several defendants (meaning allegedly at-fault parties), including NYC Bike Share, LLC (the company that operated the Citi Bike system), New York City, and the New York City Department of Transportation, for ease of explanation, I'm going to collapse all of these defendants (as well as some later-added ones) into "NYC Bike Share." Corwin alleged claims for, among other things, common-law negligence and gross negligence.

But here's the wrinkle: Corwin signed the monster waiver described previously. It checked some of the boxes we've discussed and more—releases, disclaimers, limited liability, and even assumption of risk. Plus, he signed it the exact same way all of us do—without even knowing it. And though he didn't remember signing it, NYC Bike Share testified that he couldn't have rented a bike *without* signing the clickwrap agreement containing all these ugly waivers and releases. In other words, not a good way to start his case.

Seeing as NYC Bike Share had this great waiver defense, it petitioned the court for what's called "summary judgment." That's when a defendant asks the court to toss out the plaintiff's case because the facts are so indisputably in the defendant's favor that it's not even worth troubling a jury. In particular, NYC Bike Share asked the court to throw out Corwin's claims because of its release. For Corwin's part, he asked the court to dismiss NYC Bike Share's waiver defenses. He claimed they were void because they violated public policy, meaning the public's sensibilities.

As a preliminary matter, the court had to decide whether Corwin actually signed the release. Remember, Corwin said he never remembered doing it. The court agreed with NYC Bike Share that Corwin couldn't have rented a bike had he not been a member, so his attempt to argue he never signed the release in the first place quickly fell flat.

The court next turned to the terms of the release and its enforceability—a scary prospect for Corwin because if the court ruled against him, his case would be over, and he'd never receive compensation for his serious injuries, such as payments for his medical expenses, lost wages, and pain and suffering. See how undetectable liability waivers can quickly become really big deals?

Reviewing the merits of NYC Bike Share's waiver, the court considered whether it was an unconscionable adhesion contract, as Corwin insisted. (See how the lessons I described above play out in real life?) The court observed that a waiver is an unconscionable and unenforceable adhesion contract when its formation involves "an absence of meaningful choice on the part of one of the parties together with contract terms which are unreasonably favorable to the other party." *Id.* at 488.

Noting that clickwrap agreements are "more readily enforceable than online contracts that do not require the user to take an affirmative action since they permit courts to infer that the user was at least on inquiry notice of the terms of the agreement, and has outwardly manifested consent by clicking a box," *id.* at 489, the court remarked that "courts have enforced such contracts, absent extraordinary circumstances." *Id.* This was not good language for Corwin.

That said, the court added that merely clicking through a clickwrap agreement "without more [is] insufficient to signal [a plaintiff's] assent to any contract term." *Id.* Through this language, the court leaned the other way. Arguments supporting *both* parties existed. So what did the court do?

The court looked to other cases (a process known as *stare decisis*) for a test it could use to solve this problem. And it found one, articulated by a respected federal judge in an adjacent judicial district. The court said that first, the waiver must at least be noticeable, meaning it must have at least put Corwin on "inquiry notice." *Id.*

Second, the website must be set up in such a way as to encourage the plaintiff to examine the waiver language, such as through a hyperlink. Relatedly, the waiver "should not be enforced when [it is] buried at the bottom of a webpage or tucked away in obscure corners." *Id.*

Considering the court's test, NYC Bike Share claimed that "before the prospective member [could] proceed to pay for the membership, each person is shown the…User Agreement" that was "displayed on the page in its own scrollable text box [and the membership would] not activate until Corwin clicked on a statement reading 'I certify that I am the Member, I am 18 years old or over, and I have read and agree to the conditions set forth in the User Agreement.'" *Id.* at 490.

What's more, the ten-page agreement "contained a bold-faced and underlined section in larger font titled 'Releases; Disclaimers; Limited Liability; Assumption of the Risk[,' and t]he text of the sections in question [were] in normal-sized font." *Id.*

Considering these facts against the legal test the court articulated, the court found "the Release Agreement [was] enforceable," *id.*, explaining that "[t]he full scrollable text of the agreement was available on the same page a user must utilize to register, requiring no clicking of hyperlinks, and the user couldn't continue to input his payment information until he signal[ed] assent to the agreement by taking the affirmative step of clicking a box." *Id.*

The court observed that "[w]hile it [was] possible to imagine clearer signaling of the importance of the waiver provisions to an unwary or unsophisticated consumer, the terms [were] not hidden or buried in an obscure part of the website, but rather are in plain view." *Id.* Accordingly, ruled the court, "the Release Agreement [was] not unconscionable, and Corwin [was] not entitled to [NYC Bike Share's] affirmative defenses on that basis." *Id.*

That's a pretty rotten outcome for Corwin for a waiver he never even knew he signed.

I wonder if Corwin would have worn a helmet or been more careful had he perused the clearly visible, bold sections of his contract, knowing that if anything happened to him he couldn't sue NYC Bike Share. If there's a moral to his story, that's it.

But a momentary glimmer of good news emerged from Corwin's case. The only claims he waived against NYC Bike Share were his "common-law" negligence claims. Several paragraphs above, you might have noticed that I described his negligence claim as deriving from the common law. This was a critical legal point. Common-law negligence means ordinary carelessness, not extreme carelessness, which is called gross negligence.

You'll remember I mentioned Corwin sued NYC Bike Share for *both* types of negligence. The court's ruling as to the waiver's enforceability only applied to Corwin's common-law negligence claim, *not* his gross-negligence claim. Indeed, the waiver released NYC Bike Share from negligence "except for

Claims caused by the Released Person's gross negligence or willful misconduct." *Id.* at 485.

But while this might sound like a loophole-win for Corwin, in that he still had a negligence claim in his pocket, it meant he'd need to prove that NYC Bike Share acted willfully or egregiously in causing his injury. Because none of the facts supported that finding, the court dismissed his case.

So that's a real-life example of everything this chapter is about and the potential legal pitfalls you're exposed to constantly without even knowing it. The best way to avoid being a victim is to read (or at least skim) your contracts to observe their get-out-of-jail-free language and take extra caution to avoid ending up in a situation where you have no rights.

But not every adhesion contract is for an unnecessary or elusive service like a bike in New York City. Many are for more routine services, such as health clubs and music festivals. You can't rewrite these contracts by crossing out and initialing the waiver clauses. Indeed, many contracts, such as for concert tickets, appear exclusively online, meaning you can't take a pen to them at all.

So, again, what can you do? Other than to hope against the enforceability of a waiver once it's raised against you in litigation—because it was procedurally unconscionable (meaning hidden) or substantively unconscionable (meaning really heavy-handed)—I'm afraid not much.

That's why, when an engagement requiring a waiver involves physical activity and the potential for injury (as most do, which is why vendors include waivers to begin with), you need to be extra careful. This means wearing a helmet when you rent a bike, not lifting more than you can, wearing nonslip shower shoes when you're at your health club, and avoiding the mosh pit at a concert, especially if you've had too much to drink.

Hey, it's dangerous out there—both in terms of getting hurt and your ability to do something about it. But now that you know what you're up against, you can exercise that extra ounce of prevention, which is often all that's required to keep yourself safe.

Chapter 10

The importance of having a will and trust—trust me, your family will thank you!

It's terrible when a loved one passes away. But that tragedy becomes needlessly worse when the decedent hasn't adequately planned for this inevitability. Having a will and, better yet, a trust avoids tons of heart-wrenching problems.

Before examining these necessary legal devices, let's check out what happens when you have neither a will nor a trust.

Why you need at least a will

If you die without a will, it's called dying "intestate." It's then a local probate court's job to decide how to distribute your property. And though the probate judge will follow state intestacy laws that seek to mimic the final wishes of the average person, *your* actual wishes are unknown. Sad thing is, nearly 70 percent of Americans bear this risk because they don't have a will or an up-to-date will.

So while you're alive, you need to have a will. If you don't, when you die, the distribution process goes through probate and can cost a ton in dollars and aggravation to your family members. Wills are incredibly simple to establish, though you'll need to get the forms notarized and have two witnesses present. After all, you won't be around to distribute your assets, so more than one person is necessary to attest to the accuracy of your wishes.

But even with a will, your estate may go to probate court. Probate is the legal process where a court oversees the distribution of your assets after your death. If you have a will, this process begins with its authentication and the appointment of your executor—the person you've chosen to carry out the terms of your will.

What happens to your things if you die without a will?

If you die without a will, the probate process often starts with the state naming an administrator for you. Typically, the probate judge appoints the surviving spouse or one of the decedent's adult children. Until the court appoints an administrator, your assets will be frozen. If no one wants (or is available) to serve as administrator, the court will name a public trustee to distribute your assets. This means pretty much anybody could be in charge of distributing your estate.

Whether you have a will or not, the probate judge will rely on state law to decide how to distribute your estate. Often, the probate process is slow and expensive. Things only get more complicated when you have a large or complex estate.

State intestate-succession laws determine how the probate court distributes your assets when you die without a will. It's a pretty cold and sterile process. Here are some general principles of how intestate succession works:

- Order of priority: Typically, creditors are paid first (funeral bill, credit cards, loans, mortgages, etc.). If your state has a death (estate) tax, taxes may be owed. After creditors and taxes, the order of priority for heirs is spouse, children, parents, siblings, then other close relatives.
- Assets to which intestate succession applies: Intestate succession can apply to property, vehicles, bank accounts, brokerage accounts, pets, heirlooms, 401(k) accounts, life insurance policies without beneficiaries, and more.
- Assets to which intestate succession doesn't apply: Property put in a living trust (we'll discuss trusts shortly) or that's part of a life insurance policy or retirement account with named beneficiaries.
- State law applies: The state law where you died determines which intestacy laws apply, and the probate court will open a case in the state where your main home was located. If you own property in another state, you may need a probate administration there too.
- Assets can go to the state: If there are no surviving relatives, your assets may go to the state.

But, again, if you make a will, you have more control over who will receive your property after you pass. In your last will and testament, you merely list your assets and name beneficiaries for each item. Anything you don't list will become part of your residuary estate for which you may also name a beneficiary. You can even divide your residuary among multiple beneficiaries, giving each a percentage as indicated in your will.

Dying without a will really affects your loved ones

Dying intestate will waste your loved ones' time and money, which will make their grieving process even worse. A will accomplishes several things the probate court would otherwise decide. Here are a few more pluses in addition to those I've already described:

- **Appointing your executor:** The executor of a will is the person responsible for managing your estate as it proceeds through probate. Often, the testator (meaning the person who wrote the will) names the person they want to be executor.
- **Nominating guardians for your minor children:** To me, if there were any reason to have a will, this is it. While minor children usually go to their surviving parent, you can name legal guardians to take care of your kids if you and your spouse pass away together. You certainly don't want a court-appointed administrator and probate judge to decide this.
- **Nominating caretakers for your pets:** Let's not forget the pets. Though the law considers pets "chattel," or personal property, you can nominate a caretaker for them by leaving them to someone in your will.
- **Instructions for debts and taxes:** Typically, people die with debt, whether a home loan, credit card debt, or something else. Sometimes wills include directions

for how the executor should handle debts and taxes from the estate. This removes unnecessary stress from your heirs.

- **Leaving gifts to charities:** If you're philanthropically inclined, you can leave a gift to a cause you cared about during your lifetime. To do this, your will simply names a charity as a beneficiary.
- **Distributing specific assets and property:** If you'd like to make sure your daughter has your wedding ring, you can list it as a gift to her. You can gift other heirlooms or items of sentimental value to other people by naming them as beneficiaries.
- **Distributing the rest of your property:** The rest of your property is called your "residuary estate." You can name beneficiaries to receive your residuary estate. This can cover the assets you didn't otherwise distribute.
- **Messages to beneficiaries:** Messages aren't technically part of a will. But they are a kind gesture to accompany the distribution of any gifts.

More about the kids because they're super important: If you die without a will, who will take care of them?

If you die without a will that names a guardian for your minor children and your spouse is no longer living, the court will name a guardian. The court's first choice would be the grandparents but whose? Yours or your spouse's parents whom you never liked? It could get messy fast and with no one advocating directly for your kids.

If there are no grandparents or the grandparents are unwilling or unable to take responsibility for the kids, the court turns to the next closest relative—typically, this means aunts and uncles. Among these relatives, the court has discretion to choose the best person based on the judge's estimation of the children's best interests. But the court doesn't know your kids. For this reason, plenty of nightmare scenarios could result from the judge's intervention:

- Maybe your parents are getting old but won't admit they can't suitably care for your kids.
- Maybe your parents are fine, but you and your spouse promised years ago that you'd never raise your kids the way your parents raised you.
- What if the only grandparents left are your spouse's and you never really liked them?
- What if there are no grandparents and the only person left is your sister, who drinks too much and is drowning in credit card debt that the judge doesn't know about?
- Switching directions, what if more than one family member wants to raise the kids, which puts your kids in the middle of a long and expensive court battle?
- What if you don't have any close relatives who can take the kids? The court will appoint someone else but who? This consideration gets even trickier when potential guardians live out of state.

These are just a few of the horrors concerning your kids that can easily come from not having a will. Fortunately, you can avoid all of this by having a will that accounts for them.

Summing up the pros and cons of having a will

I know that was a lot to digest, so here's a quick checklist of the pros of having a will:

1. You decide how your estate will be distributed.
2. You decide who will take care of your minor children.
3. Your family avoids a long and expensive probate process.
4. It can help minimize estate taxes.
5. You can always change your mind about your choices.

But as with anything, there are some cons (modest as they may be) associated with having a will:

1. A will can be challenged, such as by heirs who are unhappy with their take or wary of the circumstances concerning your will's creation (e.g., the ol' "someone moved dad's hand to sign while he was unconscious" routine). The test here is undue influence. A common challenge would be where dad had Alzheimer's or was on medication when an evil family member directed him to sign the new document.
2. Probate may still be required, which can be expensive and lengthy.
3. A will creates a public record, which is something not everybody's keen on.
4. A will may not minimize estate taxes to the greatest extent possible.
5. A will won't take effect until the time of death, meaning it may not account for end-of-life needs.

Why it's important to have a trust

So that's a bit on wills, but our work doesn't stop there. Now we need to talk about trusts.

Though trusts sound like a fancy concept for super-rich people, that stereotype couldn't be further from the truth. Trusts are for everyone and should be part of everyone's estate plan, no matter the amount of money they have.

The interesting twist is that having a trust isn't so much about dying as it is a process that emphasizes your surviving family members. Most people who include trusts in their estate plans do so to take care of their families, which is precisely the point of a trust. A trust achieves that goal by uniquely (and affordably) blending privacy and asset protection with the ability to avoid an expensive and lengthy probate process.

What is a trust?

A trust is a legal document that creates a three-way relationship between three different parties: the trust, its trustee, and its beneficiaries.

1. **The trust** is the legal entity that holds title to the assets inside the trust.
2. **The trustee** is the person who decides matters relating to the trust.
3. **The beneficiaries** are people who receive assets from the trust.

If you create a trust, you're called the *grantor* (or, in some states, a trustor, settlor, or creator). As grantor, you describe how the trust's assets can be used during your lifetime and how its assets will pass to your beneficiaries when you die.

Perhaps the best (and most valuable) thing about a trust is that it allows your loved ones to avoid long, public, and expensive probate court proceedings, which, as I described, can still occur when you have a will.

So don't let the word *trust* intimidate you. Before my wife and I got trusts, I was anxious about what we were getting into. But trusts aren't scary at all. They're easy to set up and available to everyone.

Why it's important to have a will with your trust

A question I sometimes hear is, "Do I need a will if I already have a trust?" The short and simple answer is yes.

The first reason is that a trust covers only property you have transferred, in writing, to the trust. Almost nobody transfers everything to their trust. And even if you do your best, there's always the chance you'll acquire property shortly before you die that you don't think to transfer or can't transfer into your trust. This means your newly acquired property won't pass under the terms of your trust.

The second reason is that a will can accomplish some important things a trust can't. As we've discussed, if you have minor children and want to name a guardian for them, you must use a will. You can't use your trust. You can also use a will to forgive (or cancel) debts owed to you.

What trusts achieve that wills don't

Beyond trusts offering your family a road map for your wishes—a wonderful gift, especially during an exceptionally sad time—trusts offer a bunch of estate-planning and asset protection benefits that wills don't.

- **Avoiding probate.** Many types of trusts avoid the expensive and public probate process.
- **Living benefits.** Many trusts allow you to stay in control of assets in the trust throughout your lifetime. Trusts can also spell out how your trustee should handle your affairs if you become incapacitated or severely sick, which can bring ease to your loved ones.
- **Potential tax benefits.** Since trusts remove assets from your estate, they can potentially help reduce estate and income taxes for your beneficiaries and preserve more of your wealth.
- **Charitable giving.** Certain trusts can help you achieve philanthropic goals.
- **Asset protection.** Trusts can help protect your assets from lawsuits, creditors, and even events like divorce.
- **Provide privacy.** Because assets held in a trust are titled in the trust's name, the grantor's and beneficiaries' names aren't a public record.

See how, despite your financial status, a trust can help create a plan during your lifetime to ensure that your assets pass as quickly as possible to your intended beneficiaries? And it can be done privately in a way that gives your family a sense of comfort.

What types of trusts exist?

Two main types of trusts exist: revocable and irrevocable. And within irrevocable trusts, lots of additional trust types exist.

1. Revocable trusts

A grantor can change or terminate a revocable trust at any time. Revocable trusts are flexible and are also known as *living trusts.*

The ability to change your trust can be meaningful if you have unexpected life changes, such as healthcare issues, a late-in-life marriage, a divorce, new children, and the like.

A revocable trust can also come in especially handy if you own property in multiple states. Let's say you own homes in Illinois and Florida. You could be subject to probate in both states. But if you own both properties inside of a revocable trust, you could avoid probate in both states, thus making the administration of your estate quicker and cheaper.

And although you have a trustee who manages the trust for you, because you can make changes to a revocable trust, you'll still be viewed as the owner of the assets. This means you'll be responsible for making tax payments and reporting the trust's investment returns. Also, a revocable trust's assets are included in your estate and are available to creditors.

Finally, you can have your revocable trust end upon your death and have all assets distributed to your beneficiaries then. But you can also set it up so that upon your passing, your revocable trust will create irrevocable trusts that continue for different people or institutions.

2. Irrevocable trusts

Unlike a revocable trust, you can't amend or terminate an irrevocable trust after you've formed it. This means you can't access any funds you've placed inside the trust until the terms of the trust have been met. The trust even pays its own income taxes and files a separate return.

Several types of irrevocable trusts exist, from common spousal trusts that you'd establish for your spouse's benefit to irrevocable life insurance trusts that hold one or more life insurance policies whose death benefits would pay to your heirs or cover the costs of administering your estate without incurring taxes.

If irrevocable trusts sound strict, you might wonder why they exist. Because they can offer certain benefits. Though assets used to fund a testamentary trust, which I'll explain in a second, may be subject to probate, the flexibility a testamentary trust offers when you want to control the assets for a period of time after you die could outweigh its costs.

For instance, let's say you put money into an irrevocable trust, which means you've relinquished control of that money. With this money removed from your estate, it now doesn't count toward the rest of your assets when it comes to calculating your potential estate taxes. If a tax benefit like this is important to you, an irrevocable trust might be the way to go.

As I mentioned, you can even set up your will or revocable trust to automatically create irrevocable trusts when you die. When you use your will to create an irrevocable trust, it's called a testamentary trust. You create a testamentary trust through a will or revocable trust, and the terms of the trust are described in the will.

Depending on your circumstances, you can choose from several types of irrevocable trusts. Indeed, your reason for setting up an irrevocable trust—wealth transfer to the next generation, keeping a family business in the family, funding an important charity, minimizing your beneficiaries' estate taxes, or shielding your assets from creditors—will inform the type that best fits your needs.

With all that explained, here are some of the different types of irrevocable trusts you can choose from, depending on your circumstances:

- **Irrevocable life insurance trusts (ILITs).** Often, an ILIT is used to set aside funds for estate taxes. You might find an ILIT especially useful if you own a family business that you'd like to remain in your estate after you pass. If so, you can create an ILIT ahead of time to ensure the business stays in your family, despite estate bills, by gifting your life insurance premiums into the ILIT each year.

  Your trustee will own the policy, and when you pass away, the trustee will collect the policy proceeds. The trustee will then distribute the proceeds to the trust's beneficiaries, who can use them to pay estate taxes. This will ensure that your beneficiaries won't have to sell the family business. Your beneficiaries could also use the proceeds to fund a buy/sell agreement where they buy out the remaining owners once you pass, so they can control the company.

- **Grantor-retained annuity trusts (GRATs) and qualified personal residence trusts (QPRTs).** Certain irrevocable trusts are intended to last for only a specific term of years. Two examples are grantor-retained annuity trusts (GRATs) and qualified personal residence trusts (QPRTs).

GRATs are a common way to minimize taxes on financial gifts to beneficiaries. With a GRAT, you contribute assets to your trust and receive a regular annuity payment, usually a set percentage of the original asset amount.

When the terms of the trust end, any remaining funds, including appreciation, transfer to your beneficiaries gift-tax free. If you're no longer alive when the terms end, the assets become part of the estate and are subject to estate tax.

QPRTs are another way to transfer assets—more specifically, real estate—to your beneficiaries. For instance, if you want to give your home to your child but aren't planning to move out anytime soon, you could set up a QPRT for, say, fifteen years. If you're still alive when the trust terminates, your home passes to your child outside of your estate.

These strategies leverage time and appreciation to get assets out of your estate with the goal of saving money on your estate taxes.

- **Charitable remainder annuity trusts.** If you're interested in leaving a lasting legacy, a charitable remainder annuity trust can help. You can set up this trust so the primary beneficiaries (for example, your kids) receive income to start, and a charity you choose gets any remaining assets.

Or you could flip the script and have the charity first receive income from the trust. Then, after a certain period of time, the trust would terminate, and the remaining assets would go to your kids. You might also be able to take a tax deduction for setting up this type of trust for a charitable donation.

- **Special needs trusts.** If you have a child or family member with a disability, you might consider setting up a special needs trust. Though special needs trusts are typically created for people who are eligible for government benefits due to disability, a special needs trust can provide for that person in addition to government assistance.

  Worth noting is that gifting money to a child with special needs outside of a special needs trust could disqualify them from receiving supplemental security income. But with a special needs trust, you can provide for your child while ensuring that they still qualify for government benefits.

- **Domestic asset protection trust (DAPT).** You can use a DAPT (also called a self-settled trust) to protect assets from future creditors, though it's not an option in every state. Some people set up a DAPT for their kids so assets stay in the family in the event of a divorce, meaning the spouse wouldn't have a claim to the assets.

- **Generation-skipping trusts (GST).** Often, people choose a GST for tax reasons. For instance, a GST would allow you to designate assets to your grandchildren, skipping your kids to bypass estate taxes that would occur if your kids directly inherited your assets.

These are just some of the several types of trusts available. As you can see, it's dense but not incomprehensible. As you can also see, an ounce of prevention can be worth many pounds of cure.

A very sad (and expensive) story involving yours truly

Considering my penchant for personalizing things, allow me to channel a sad story involving a lack of proper estate planning that involved me in an exceptionally sad, expensive, and painful way.

Several years ago, my aunt in Minneapolis passed away suddenly. She was unmarried and had no kids. Her closest kin were my brother and me. She had accrued a tidy sum, and her estate was meaningful. But she had only a will—no trust. Worse yet, the man she appointed executor was the person who drafted it. He was her ex-boyfriend with whom she'd had a bitter breakup. Unfortunately, she never got around to appointing a new executor.

As we now know, because my aunt had a will, it needed to go through probate court—the long and expensive process that having a trust would have avoided. The expense, in this case, went largely to my aunt's executor—the antagonistic ex-boyfriend—meaning the more time the will took to probate, the more of my aunt's estate's money the executor could pocket.

In addition to all this was the grouchy, insensitive, and overworked probate judge. Not only do courts work with meager accountability or oversight, but also the executor and judge were pals. This made it all but impossible to challenge anything the executor did. For instance, when the executor decided to sell my aunt's jewelry and car, we were largely helpless to stop him. The executor even changed the locks on her home, so I couldn't account for her possessions.

To try to keep the executor (and the process) honest, we had to hire our own attorney to appear at probate hearings. So in addition to the estate, which would ultimately go to my brother and me, while paying the executor $450/hour, we had to pay *our* lawyer $400/hour. And, of course, all the ugly challenges played themselves out in open court and on the record.

This tumult made my aunt's passing all the more painful. Had she merely updated her estate-planning documents with a trust that named my brother or me as trustee, we could have avoided everything I just described.

So please, don't let this situation or something similar happen to you. It needn't if you simply have a will and a trust. When you know what you want your trust to achieve, including how it will affect future generations, you can work with your estate-planning lawyer to decide which type of trust makes the most sense for you.

And if all that weren't enough, here's another essential document: a living will

A living will is a legal document that describes the type of medical care you want to receive if you can't make medical decisions for yourself. This can arise if you're terminally ill, in a coma, or permanently unconscious.

Living wills are one of the most common types of advance directives. They can help ensure that you receive the care you want if you can't communicate your wishes.

A living will can include instructions for such things as a dialysis machine, feeding tube, breathing tube, CPR, organ or tissue donation, and the like.

Living wills vary by state, but all fifty states allow them. State laws vary regarding the terminology, requirements, and procedures for living wills. For example, some states call these documents "living wills," while others use terms like "advance healthcare directives" or "medical directives."

People began to take more notice of living wills following several high-profile legal cases, the most famous of which involved Karen Ann Quinlan. When she was thirty-one, she became unconscious after consuming Valium with alcohol while on a crash diet. She lapsed into a coma, followed by a persistent vegetative state.

Because she had no living will, when her parents requested doctors disconnect her ventilator, they refused and her parents filed suit to disconnect her. They believed keeping her connected constituted extraordinary means of prolonging her life.

Eventually, the court ruled that the ventilator could be withdrawn. But when it was, Karen continued to breathe on her own and survived another nine years in a persistent vegetative state.

The court's ruling was precedential. It set guidelines for when doctors could agree to the pleas of terminally ill patients' relatives and withhold extraordinary measures to keep these patients alive. The case also led to the requirement that hospitals, nursing homes, and hospices have ethics committees.

For our purposes, the case led to the creation of living wills, documenting someone's personal wishes regarding the choice of using extraordinary means to maintain their life if there is no hope of recovery and they want to die with dignity. In this manner, a living will means no one has to be under the personal burden of making end-of-life decisions for a loved one.

If that story doesn't demonstrate why having a living will is essential, nothing will. All adults should make a living will regardless of their age or health. And though most people agree that having a living will is a good idea, very few adults actually have one. Like most disasters, you don't expect them, so why wait till one strikes, and it's too late? Don't you think Karen Ann Quinlan and her family wish *she'd* had a living will?

Durable power of attorney for healthcare

A durable power of attorney (POA) for healthcare is another important legal document for your estate-planning bundle. It allows you to designate someone—your agent—to make healthcare decisions for you if you can't make them yourself. A POA is durable if it states it will remain in effect if the principal becomes incapacitated. This means the agent's authority continues even if the principal can no longer make their own decisions. A POA that is not durable, or a "non-durable" POA, ends if the principal becomes incapacitated.

This document helps people plan for medical emergencies and declining mental capacity. Though a POA and a living will are similar, they're not the same thing. At a high level, a living will explicitly states your wishes concerning medical treatments and decisions. A POA grants authority to someone you trust to act on your behalf. Many people will want to have both documents because a living will applies only in limited end-of-life situations, whereas a POA covers all other situations concerning your medical care when you can't make healthcare decisions for yourself.

If you're considering a POA—and you should be—here are some things to know:

- **Who can be your agent?** Your agent can be anyone over eighteen who is not a doctor or other healthcare provider. Often, it's a spouse, family member, friend, or spiritual advisor.
- **When can your agent make decisions?** Your agent can make decisions when your attending physician determines you are no longer able to make informed healthcare decisions.
- **What can your agent do?** Your agent can decide when to start and stop treatments, undergo tests and surgery, and enroll in hospice. They can also obtain your protected healthcare information.
- **Can you have multiple agents?** You can appoint more than one agent, such as co-agents or successive agents, but this can lead to confusion or conflict, such as if the healthcare provider can only reach one agent in an emergency.
- **What happens if you also have a living will?** If you have a POA and a living will, the living will won't be overruled.

Statutory durable power of attorney

Another important POA for your estate plan is the statutory durable power of attorney. This POA springs from certain states' laws—or statutes—and it addresses different issues than a healthcare POA. (You'll have to check your state to see if it has a statute providing for a durable POA.)

A statutory durable POA appoints an agent to make certain *financial* decisions for you if you're unable to do so. Importantly, you can't use this POA for healthcare—hence, the need also for a durable POA for healthcare.

When you fill out a statutory durable POA, you'll be able to decide (1) who your agents will be, (2) what powers they'll have, and (3) when their POA becomes effective—immediately or upon your disability or incapacity. You may also limit or extend the powers you grant to your agent.

A review of certain states' statutes that provide for a statutory durable POA result in this list of powers you can choose from when filling out your statutory durable POA form:

- Real property transactions
- Tangible personal property transactions
- Stock and bond transactions
- Commodity and option transactions
- Banking and other financial institution transactions
- Business operating transactions
- Insurance and annuity transactions
- Estate, trust, and other beneficiary transactions
- Claims and litigation
- Personal and family maintenance

- Benefits from social security, Medicare, Medicaid, or other governmental programs or civil or military service
- Retirement plan transactions
- Tax matters
- Digital assets and the content of electronic communications

Totally different responsibilities than you'd grant to your durable healthcare POA. But, again, you can't address medical decisions—including the type of care you'll want to receive if you become incapacitated—through a statutory power of attorney. You'll need to accomplish this through your durable healthcare POA.

Here's an example demonstrating why a durable statutory power of attorney is vital to protecting your interests when you can't make decisions for yourself: Let's say (and I hate to say it) you get into an accident and end up in a coma. Grisly, I know. If you've signed a statutory durable POA, your agent (your child, perhaps) would have the power to make important financial and legal decisions for you. This means paying your bills, paying your taxes, and tending to any legal matters, all of which would spare your family from logistical pain when already suffering emotional pain.

Considered from the other end, if you *don't* have a statutory durable POA and you become disabled or incapacitated, you *won't* have a say in how these matters get handled or who will handle them. This means you may have to go to court and have a guardian appointed to handle your financial and legal matters. This takes time and costs money and for no good reason.

Nice thing is, you can fashion a durable statutory POA to suit any situation, meaning you can choose the breadth of your agent's powers. This flexibility lets you pick a scope and solution that works for you and protects your assets.

One of the most critical aspects of any POA document is setting it up when you—or your loved one—is of sound mind. A POA that is signed when a person is mentally incompetent is not valid. And don't worry, you can update it as necessary due to life changes, such as changing the agent following a marriage or divorce.

Because your durable statutory POA becomes effective only upon your disability or incapacity, you'd better set it up early. This means if you don't have one in place and you become incapacitated, it's too late, and your family will have to go through an expensive legal process where they ask the court to appoint a guardian. Being proactive can avoid this expense, involve someone you trust, and give your family members the peace of mind they deserve, even if they don't know you've done so.

Pet trusts

Plenty of us think of our pets as family. I know I do. We have a mini goldendoodle, Joy, and had an old Labrador retriever, Bea. Sadly, Bea moved on about a year before I wrote this book. For that reason, we want to ensure that Joy receives uninterrupted love and affection if we're no longer able to give it to her. One way to plan for that possibility is to set up a pet trust. Yep, you heard me—a pet trust.

A pet trust is a legally recognized arrangement providing for your pet's care and maintenance if you—the grantor (just as with the other trusts we discussed)—become disabled or die. Your trustee will hold money in trust for the benefit of your pets, which is payable to a caregiver you designate, such as your pet's new parents.

Why would you need a pet trust?

The scenario is simple, straightforward, and often overlooked. Let's say you and your spouse or partner (if you have one) pass away. What happens to your pet who's waiting at home?

Sure, a friend could immediately step in. But what happens when the food and vet bills start to mount? What if your friend can't afford these expenditures? Or what if your friend only has the capacity to care for your pet for a short period of time because their home is small, they have other pets to care for, or they travel for work?

Is it your friend's job to find a suitable alternative? This could be a real project that they didn't sign up for when they stepped in to care for your pet. All of these uncertainties and inconveniences are precisely why you need to plan ahead of time for what happens to your pet, which is not much different than planning for what happens to your minor children.

As we know, trusts are legally enforceable arrangements. This means pet owners can rest assured that their directions regarding their pets will be carried out. And your pet trust can be very specific. For example, if your dog only likes a particular brand of dog food or you want your cat to visit the vet quarterly, you can say so.

If you want to get extra creative, your trust can take effect during your life and can provide instructions for the care of your pet if you become incapacitated. And because you know your pet's habits better than anyone, your trust can describe the kind of care your pet should have, listing the person (or people) who'd be willing to provide that care and setting aside money for this person (or people) to provide it.

Information you'll need to set up a pet trust

In addition to providing the names and addresses of a trustee, successor trustee, caregiver, and successor caregiver, setting up a pet trust requires the following:

- Identify your pet through photos, microchips, and DNA samples. You can also describe your pet as a "class," such as, "the pets you own at the time of your illness or death."
- Describe your pet's standard of living and care.
- Determine the amount of money needed to cover your pet's expenses (generally, this amount can't exceed what's reasonably required to maintain your pet's standard of living) and describe how the money should be distributed to the caregiver.
- Determine the amount of money needed to cover the expenses of administering your pet trust.
- Designate a remainder beneficiary if the money in the pet trust isn't exhausted.
- Provide instructions for your pet's final disposition—for example, burial or cremation.

***

Morbid as it sounds, death comes neither easily nor cheap. But it only gets more difficult and more complicated if you haven't prepared for it. Nothing I've described is difficult or that expensive. It's really a matter of paying a little now or potentially a lot later. Considering this choice, it shouldn't be difficult to make the right one.

Chapter 11
Fighting back against forced-arbitration clauses

Do you own a cell phone? How about a credit card? Do you have Internet service? If you do—and you do—it means you agreed to a "forced-arbitration clause." That means when one of these vendors overcharges you, underdelivers on what was agreed to, or otherwise wrongs you, you can't take them to court. Instead, you forfeit your Seventh Amendment right to a jury trial and must submit to a secret, binding tribunal where the company that wronged you picks the decision-maker.

Worse still, many forced-arbitration clauses include a class-action ban. This means you must handle your small (but important) claim on your own. This all but ensures that no lawyer will be willing to take your case.

If forced arbitration is so patently anticonsumer, let's discuss why forced-arbitration clauses are so prevalent.

How does forced arbitration arise, and what does a forced-arbitration clause look like?

There's no sense in discussing the forced-arbitration clauses hidden in your consumer contracts unless I let you know how one arises in real life and what a typical clause looks like.

Recently, some friends of mine took an Alaskan cruise. Feast your eyes on the mess that befell them, as chronicled in the letter I wrote to the cruise line for them:

> Captain Merrill Stubing
> Senior Manager, Guest Relations
> Love Boat Cruise Lines
> 568 Love Boat Way
> Boca Raton, FL 33433
>
> RE: Passengers: Bert Convy and Florence Henderson
> Love Boat Booking No.: 584A4T
> Trip: Denali National Park
> Date of incident: July 6, 2024
>
> Dear Captain Stubing,
>
> My clients Bert Convy and Florence Henderson recently retired and were looking forward to their cruise/land experience on the Love Boat. Indeed, for years they'd planned their trip. They began their adventure in Alaska and thoroughly enjoyed the cruise portion. But their good time came to an abrupt halt with the commencement of the land portion.

On July 10, Mr. Convy received an onboard communication regarding a fire in Denali National Park, where the land portion of my clients' excursion was to commence. The communication explained that the park was closed, so he contacted the airline and moved up their flights home, aligning them with the end of their cruise portion of the trip instead of the end of their land portion. This schedule change cost them $400.

The next day, Mr. Convy received another on-board communication, this one explaining that the land portion of the cruise was still proceeding. But the communication contained the following ambiguous statement: "[T]here may be some changes to your itinerary during your trip, which may include access to Denali National Park."

Considering that they only wanted the land portion if they could enter the park, Mr. Convy met with guest services, seeking definite information about access to the park. The representative assured him the park was open.

Despite this assurance, Mr. Convy did not change back their flights. To make even more certain that the park would be open, he visited guest services the next day. As occurred the day before, the representative assured him the park would be open, and their tour would proceed as planned.

Based on both guest services representatives' assurances, he changed back their flights. This change cost them another $450.

When they arrived at McKinley Chalet the next day, the hotel clerk told them the park was closed. My clients (and hundreds of other passengers) were livid.

With the unexpected cancellation of the Denali tour, my clients had no other plans. As avid hikers, they'd been eager to spend time on the trails, but now they had to scramble to fill their schedule with the few non-Denali excursions available, all of which were in short supply and extremely expensive.

The Love Boat could have avoided all this by simply telling my clients the park was closed instead of doubling down and claiming—indeed, defrauding my clients into believing—it was open. Indeed, the Love Boat left hundreds of passengers angry and with dashed vacations.

My clients would not have stayed and spent money on the land portion of their cruise had they known Denali was closed. In addition to the $850 they unnecessarily paid to change

> their flights, the land portion of their cruise that was not as advertised cost them $2,500.
>
> The Love Boat offered them $100 for their troubles. This amount is insufficient. Instead, I am demanding the Love Boat pay my clients $5,000 within ten days of this letter's mailing date. If they don't receive payment by this time, they will commence a lawsuit against the Love Boat, alleging breach of contract and fraud. They will also consider the possibility of filing a nationwide class-action lawsuit in federal court.
>
> I look forward to your anticipated cooperation.
>
> Best personal regards.
>
> Very truly yours,
> *s/Daniel R. Karon*
> Daniel R. Karon

Seems like a pretty cut-and-dried screw over, right? Unfortunately, not so fast. Buried toward the end of the cruise line's online contract, in Paragraph 17, was a forced-arbitration clause. Decked out with all the available bells and whistles, it was one of the ugliest forced-arbitration clauses I'd ever seen, and it went on and on. Brace yourself because this resembles the forced-arbitration clauses buried in almost all of *your* consumer contracts.

The language we're centering on begins at section (B)(ii), but I've included the preceding language for context and completeness:

17. NOTICE OF CLAIMS AND ACTIONS; TIME LIMITATION; ARBITRATION; FORUM; WAIVER OF CLASS ACTION; WAIVER OF RIGHT TO IN REM PROCEDURES OF ARREST AND ATTACHMENT.

The following provisions are for the benefit of the Carrier and certain third-party beneficiaries as set forth above in Section 1:

(A) Notice of Claims and Time Limits for Legal Action:

(i) Claims for Injury, Illness or Death: In cases involving claims for emotional harm, bodily injury, illness to or death of any Guest, no lawsuit may be brought against Carrier unless (1) written notice giving full particulars of the claim is delivered to Carrier within 6 months from the date of the emotional harm, bodily injury, illness or death, (2) a lawsuit on such a claim is filed within 1 year from the date of the injury, illness or death, and (3) valid service of the lawsuit is made within 90 days of filing the complaint.

(ii) All Other Claims: No claim of any kind, including without limitation alleged violations of civil rights, discrimination, consumer or privacy laws, or other statutory, constitutional or legal rights, or for any losses, damages or expenses relating to or in any way arising out of or connected with this Cruise Contract or Guest's cruise, Land Trips and/or Air Package, other than for emotional or bodily injury, illness or death of any Guest, shall be brought against Carrier unless (1) written notice giving full particulars of the claim is delivered to the Carrier within 15 days of the actual or scheduled termination date of the Cruise, or post-cruise Land Trip, whichever occurs first as specified in connection with this Contract, (2) legal action on such claim is commenced within 1 year from such scheduled termination date, and (3) valid notice or service of any such action is effected upon Carrier within 90 days after commencement of the action.

(B) Forum and Jurisdiction for Legal Action:

(i) <u>Claims for Injury, Illness or Death</u>: All claims or disputes involving emotional harm, bodily injury, illness to or death of any Guest whatsoever including without limitation those arising out of or relating to this Cruise Contract or Your Cruise, Land Trip(s), or Air Package shall be litigated in and before the United States District Court for the Southern District of Florida at West Palm Beach, or as to those lawsuits over which the Federal Courts of the United States lack subject matter jurisdiction, before a court located in Palm Beach County, State of Florida, U.S.A., to the exclusion of the courts of any other country, state, city, municipality, county or locale. You consent to jurisdiction and waive any objection that may be available to any such action being brought in such courts.

(ii) All Other Claims; Agreement to Arbitrate: All claims other than for emotional harm, bodily injury, illness to or death of a Guest, whether based on contract, tort, statutory, constitutional or other legal rights, including without limitation alleged violations of civil rights, discrimination, consumer or privacy laws, or for any losses, damages or expenses, relating to or in any way arising out of or connected with this Cruise Contract or Guest's cruise, Land Trip(s), and/or Air Package, with the sole exception of claims brought and litigated in small claims court, shall be referred to and resolved exclusively by binding arbitration pursuant to the United Nations Convention on the Recognition and Enforcement of Foreign Arbitral Awards (New York, 1958), 21 U.S.T. 2517, 330 U.N.T.S. 3, 1970 U.S.T. LEXIS 115, 9 U.S.C. §§ 202-208 ("the Convention") and the Federal Arbitration Act, 9 U.S.C. § 1 et seq., ("FAA") located in Palm Beach County, State of Florida, U.S.A. to the exclusion of any other forum. You agree that the arbitrator shall resolve any dispute as to the validity or applicability of this arbitration clause. You consent to jurisdiction and waive any objection that may be available to any such arbitration proceeding in Palm Beach County, Florida.

The arbitration shall be administered by US Arbitration and Association ("USAA") under its Comprehensive Dispute Resolution Rules and Procedures and the fee schedule in effect at the time of initiating the proceeding with USAA, which are deemed to be incorporated herein by reference. The arbitration shall proceed live at USAA's offices, located at 754 Lexington Ave., Suite 3400, New York City, NY 10166. The parties shall each be responsible for half of the initial fee of $3,500.

Contact USAA to respond to any questions regarding the arbitration process or to obtain a current copy of the Comprehensive Dispute Resolution Rules and Procedures and/or fee schedule. The arbitrator must follow this Contract and can award the same damages and relief as a court.

NEITHER PARTY WILL HAVE THE RIGHT TO A JURY TRIAL OR TO ENGAGE IN PRE-ARBITRATION DISCOVERY EXCEPT AS PROVIDED IN THE APPLICABLE ARBITRATION RULES AND HEREIN, OR OTHERWISE TO LITIGATE THE CLAIM IN ANY COURT (OTHER THAN SMALL CLAIMS COURT). THE ARBITRATOR'S

> DECISION WILL BE FINAL AND BINDING. OTHER RIGHTS (C) THAT YOU OR CARRIER WOULD HAVE IN COURT ALSO MAY NOT BE AVAILABLE IN ARBITRATION.

An award rendered by an arbitrator may be entered in any court having jurisdiction under the Convention or FAA.

Carrier and Guest agree that each shall have the right to take one (1) deposition of a witness or a party and only one deposition of an expert designated by another party. Such depositions shall be limited to three (3) hours each. The parties further agree that each party shall be permitted to propound to another party a single document production request no more than ten (10) specific categories of documents that are material as evidence in the case.

In addition, each party may propound only one set of interrogatories to another party containing no more than twenty-five (25) interrogatories, including all subparts. Upon request by a party, the arbitrator(s) shall have the power to order such discovery, by way of document production, interrogatory, deposition or otherwise, as the arbitrator(s) considers necessary for a full and fair exploration of the issues in dispute.

All claims filed in small claims court, and any claim as to which this arbitration provision is deemed unenforceable or which cannot be arbitrated for reasons beyond Your control, shall be litigated in and before the United States

District Court for the Southern District of Florida at West Palm Beach, or as to those lawsuits over which the Federal Courts of the United States lack subject matter jurisdiction, before a court located in Palm Beach County, State of Florida, U.S.A., to the exclusion of the courts of any other country, state, city, municipality, county or locale. You consent to jurisdiction and waive any objection that may be available to any such action or proceeding being brought in such courts.

The Arbitrator(s) and not any federal, state or local court or agency, shall have exclusive authority to resolve any dispute relating to the interpretation, applicability, enforceability or formation of this agreement to Arbitrate including, but not limited to any claim that all or any part of this agreement to Arbitrate is void or voidable.

(C) **WAIVER OF CLASS ACTION**: THIS CRUISE CONTRACT PROVIDES FOR THE EXCLUSIVE RESOLUTION OF DISPUTES THROUGH INDIVIDUAL LEGAL ACTION ON YOUR OWN BEHALF INSTEAD OF THROUGH ANY CLASS OR REPRESENTATIVE ACTION. EVEN IF THE APPLICABLE LAW PROVIDES OTHERWISE, YOU AGREE THAT ANY ARBITRATION OR LAWSUIT AGAINST CARRIER WHATSOEVER SHALL BE LITIGATED BY YOU INDIVIDUALLY AND NOT AS A MEMBER OF ANY CLASS OR AS PART OF A CLASS OR REPRESENTATIVE

> ACTION, AND YOU EXPRESSLY AGREE TO WAIVE ANY LAW ENTITLING YOU TO PARTICIPATE IN A CLASS ACTION. IF YOUR CLAIM IS SUBJECT TO ARBITRATION UNDER SECTION 17(B)(ii) ABOVE, THE ARBITRATOR SHALL HAVE NO AUTHORITY TO ARBITRATE CLAIMS ON A CLASS ACTION BASIS.
>
> YOU AGREE THAT THIS CLASS ACTION WAIVER SHALL NOT BE SEVERABLE UNDER ANY CIRCUMSTANCES FROM THE ARBITRATION CLAUSE SET FORTH IN SECTION 17(B)(ii) ABOVE, AND IF FOR ANY REASON THIS CLASS ACTION WAIVER IS UNENFORCEABLE AS TO ANY PARTICULAR CLAIM, THEN AND ONLY THEN SUCH CLAIM SHALL NOT BE SUBJECT TO ARBITRATION.

What did this sprawling, one-sided language mean for my friends' claim? We'll get to that in a minute.

Just what is forced arbitration?

That's an actual, real-life, forced-arbitration clause. It's long, but it's important for you to recognize all aspects of it. Let's unpack it because you deserve to know about the types of terms that bind you again and again. Terms that, until now, you likely didn't know you screwed you.

That's because vendors and other service providers bury these mandatory clauses in the fine print of cell phone, credit card, nursing home, and all sorts of other contracts, knowing you won't read the stuff. If you don't believe me, just go to your cell phone provider's online terms and conditions, press Ctrl-F and type "arbitration." You'll bristle at what you see.

Increasingly, corporations are using forced-arbitration clauses in their contracts' fine print to shield themselves from accountability in the courts. Indeed, this practice is so widespread that it's almost impossible to do anything these days without agreeing to forced arbitration. Whether keeping details about dangerous products out of the public eye or keeping people facing workplace discrimination quiet, corporations use arbitration in sweeping and dangerous ways to wipe away our access to the courts.

Just by purchasing a phone, applying for a credit card, or buying the scads of other products or services we all do, you're forced to give up your right to go to court if the company you're dealing with harms you. And I say "forced to give up" instead of merely "*that* you give up" because if you want a cell phone, credit card, or even a job, you have no choice but to agree to an ugly forced-arbitration clause.

And why? Because virtually every company offering these services includes forced-arbitration clauses in their contracts.

Remember when describing liability waivers, we discussed adhesion (or take-it-or-leave-it) contracts? The same adhesion contracts that include these nasty liability waivers also include forced-arbitration clauses. And because the private system of forced arbitration benefits companies (just as liability waivers do), companies are all too eager to slip them into your agreements, the content of which you don't notice any more than you don't notice your adhesion contracts' liability waivers—at least till it's too late.

But make no mistake, forced arbitration isn't limited to products and services. These days, many employers include a forced-arbitration agreement in their employment contract or employee handbook that you must agree to as a term of employment. If you don't agree to the terms of your contract or employee handbook (say, you find a forced-arbitration clause in your contract and attempt to strike it), the company simply won't hire you.

Here's a personal case in point. Recently, my son graduated from college and started at his first job. When he received his offer, he also received an email containing a link to several employment documents, one of which was an employment agreement that contained—you guessed it—a forced-arbitration clause. It required him to arbitrate any disputes, such as wage claims, which we'll discuss in Chapter 16, instead of submitting these disputes to a jury of his peers as the Seventh Amendment to the US Constitution allows. He had no idea what forced arbitration was, and I had the displeasure of explaining it to him. He asked me how that could be legal. I told him "Welcome to the working world."

If you don't think forced arbitration is a huge deal in the workplace, think back to Fox News anchor Gretchen Carlson's sexual harassment suit against Roger Ailes, the then-CEO of the network. Her lawsuit triggered revelations of other high-profile sexual assault scandals in the media industry and helped to propel the #MeToo movement.

Her employment contract with Fox News included a forced-arbitration clause that barred her from suing her employer. So how did she get around it? After all, I just said she *sued* her employer, which means she proceeded in court. Uniquely, Carlson's lawyers crafted a legal theory against Ailes *personally* under New York City Human Rights Law, a strategy that will rarely be available to consumers. Fox News ended up paying her a $20 million settlement.

But what about other employees who have similar claims? About 60 million workers (more than half of the nonunionized private-sector workforce) are subject to forced-arbitration agreements. Many of these agreements also require workers to waive the right to bring class-action claims and prohibit them from disclosing or discussing their complaints.

A growing body of empirical research suggests that workers are disadvantaged by being forced into arbitration. As #MeToo highlighted the ongoing pervasiveness of sexual harassment, advocates argued that forced arbitration and nondisclosure policies contributed to this problem by forcing complaints into private arbitrations rather than public court filings.

Because of these concerns—as well as the publicity associated with Carlson's lawsuit—Congress passed, and President Biden signed, the Ending Forced Arbitration of Sexual Assault and Sexual Harassment Act. The Act bars the use of forced-arbitration clauses in employment contracts and takes survivors' (like Carlson's) claims out of the private arbitration process that employers used to shield themselves. A big victory for victims, to be sure.

But if forced arbitration troubled Congress enough to pass this act relating to employment issues, it stands to reason Congress has also passed a law proscribing this same ugly forced arbitration in more general commercial settings, right? Wrong!

Remember, Congress was politically motivated to pass the Act due, in part, to the #MeToo movement.

But no such movement relates to consumer concerns. That's why the Forced Arbitration Injustice Repeal (FAIR) Act, which would prohibit the validity of predispute, forced-arbitration agreements in consumer or civil rights claims against corporations, has never cleared the Senate. This means that, for now, forced-arbitration clauses are here to stay as they pertain to everyday consumer issues.

Where did forced arbitration even come from?

The scourge that is forced arbitration began with *Concepcion v. AT&T Mobility*, 563 U.S. 333 (2011), a five-to-four decision by the US Supreme Court that dramatically altered the law on class-action arbitration and the way businesses contract with consumers. *The New York Times* described *Concepcion* as a "devastating blow to consumer rights"[3] because the ruling allows companies insulation from accountability via boilerplate language banning consumers from pursuing their claims in court—instead banishing them to arbitration.

The dispute in *Concepcion* involved a cell phone contract between Liza and Vincent Concepcion and AT&T. Lured by AT&T's promise of "free" cell phones, the Concepcions bought a two-year service contract only to later learn they needed to pay $30.22 in sales taxes. For the alleged bait and switch, they filed a class-action lawsuit. After all, a class action was the only economical way to pursue their admittedly low-value claim.

Putting aside what you might think about the merits of the Concepcions' case, they alleged AT&T had engaged in false advertising and fraud by charging sales tax on what were supposed to be entirely free cell phones. AT&T petitioned (or

---

3 Editorial, "Gutting Class Action: The Five Conservatives of the Supreme Court Chose Corporations Over Everyone Else," *The New York Times*, May 13, 2011, A26, https://www.nytimes.com/2011/05/13/opinion/13fri1.html.

moved, as lawyers call it) the court to compel arbitration under the arbitration clause in its service agreement that prohibited customers from bringing class-action arbitrations. Instead, the clause required consumers to bring individual claims in arbitration.

The district court ruled that AT&T's class-arbitration ban was unenforceable under California law. Though the district court found the arbitration agreement an adequate substitute for consumers seeking a class action, it concluded the class waiver was invalid as unconscionable under California's *Discover Bank* rule that classified as unconscionable class arbitration waivers in consumer contracts of adhesion that would exempt companies from accountability for "cheat[ing] large numbers of consumers out of individually small sums of money." *Id.* at 340 (quoting *Discover Bank v. Superior Court*, 113 P.3d 1100, 1110 (Cal. 2005)).

Dissatisfied with the district court's ruling that its class-arbitration clause was unenforceable as unconscionable, AT&T appealed to the Ninth Circuit Court of Appeals. But the Ninth Circuit affirmed the district court, agreeing that the class-arbitration waiver was unconscionable and unenforceable under California's *Discover Bank* rule.

Even more unhappy now, AT&T petitioned for *certiorari* (or review) to the US Supreme Court, which the Court granted. (Rarely a good sign for victims.) AT&T's question for the Court was whether the Federal Arbitration Act (FAA), 9 U.S.C. §§ 1-16, 201–208, and 301–307 (1925), "prohibits States from conditioning the enforceability of certain arbitration agreements on the availability of classwide arbitration procedures." *Concepcion*, 563 U.S at 336.

Writing for the majority, Justice Antonin Scalia clarified the scope of the FAA, emphasizing the Court's well-established trend of enforcing arbitration agreements. He explained that Congress enacted the FAA in 1925 as a response to state courts' reluctance to enforce commercial arbitration agreements. Over the last several decades, he wrote, the Court had interpreted the FAA broadly, instructing that any doubts concerning the scope of arbitrable issues should be resolved in favor of arbitration.

Consistent with this trend favoring the enforcement of arbitration clauses, the Court reversed the lower courts and upheld the validity of AT&T's class-arbitration waiver and such bans generally, ruling that the FAA's liberal policy favoring arbitration preempted California's *Discover Bank* rule that made class-arbitration waivers unenforceable in consumer contracts.

Never mind that Congress enacted the FAA to address business-to-business disputes, where both sides were presumably sophisticated, had the opportunity to seek counsel's assistance, and accordingly, *knew* they had agreed to resolve their disputes in private arbitration—characteristics that bore no resemblance to the Concepcions' dispute with AT&T—this was the Court's patently anticonsumer ruling.

Yet in reaching the Court's decision, Justice Scalia lauded the fairness, efficiency, and low cost of arbitration and emphasized the risk that litigation caused to defendants who would be forced to settle questionable claims. And though acknowledging the dissent's concern that "class proceedings are necessary to prosecute small-dollar claims that might otherwise slip through the legal system," *id.* at 351, Justice Scalia countered simply and conclusorily that "States cannot require a procedure that is inconsistent with the FAA." *Id.*

Immediately following the Court's ruling, countless companies introduced forced-arbitration clauses into their small print. (You'll notice *Concepcion* not only legalized forced arbitration but also banned class actions in arbitration—a clause referred to as a "class-action waiver." After we finish unpacking the more generally troubling concept of forced arbitration, we'll turn to relatedly disturbing class-action waivers.) These days, companies routinely implement forced-arbitration clauses, and courts regularly cite *Concepcion* as the reason for dismissing consumer claims in favor of forced arbitration.

Why is forced-arbitration so dangerous to consumers, and how does it differ from court?

1. Forced arbitration favors big corporations—not you.

To begin with, almost no consumers know what forced arbitration is or that they've "agreed" to it in nearly every consumer contract they've signed. Companies prefer forced arbitration because it benefits them. After all, because the defendant company often picks and pays for the arbitrator (forced-arbitration clauses commonly include these terms), the data show that the company wins about 93 percent of the time. Indeed, were the outcome otherwise, companies would stop hiring the arbitrators.

If that inherent problem weren't bad enough, here are several additional dangers and concerns highlighting why forced arbitration is so unfair to consumers:

- **Forced arbitration severely limits consumers' options for resolving disputes.** Before a problem even arises, you've locked yourself into forced arbitration without the possibility of pursuing your claim in court. Worse yet, your contract often names the arbitration company you must use, which the defendant (not you) chose. Sometimes your contract requires you to pay half the cost of arbitration. This could amount to several thousand dollars you wouldn't have to pay in court, where filing fees are typically only a few hundred dollars. Some arbitration clauses even require you to arbitrate in person at a location far from your home.

- **Typically, forced-arbitration clauses bind you but not your vendor.** Many vendors write their forced-arbitration clauses in a way that allows them to retain their right to take any complaint to court, while you can only initiate arbitration.
- **Forced-arbitration clauses prevent employees from suing their employers for discrimination, wrongful termination, or retaliation.** In forced arbitration, the laws that protect us from discrimination based on age, sex, religion, race, disability, and unequal pay for equal work, such as the Civil Rights Act and the Equal Pay Act, become unenforceable in court. Instead, you must resolve your grievances before a bought-and-paid-for arbitrator hired by your employer, who craves repeat business. This also means employees lose statutory protections for blowing the whistle on corporate waste or fraud. Similarly, employees lose the ability to fight their employers' retaliation for denying them family medical leave.
- **Consumers can't sue for negligence, defective products, or corporate scams.** Consumers can lose their right to hold a company legally accountable just by buying a product or service or even signing up for an app.

> This means if your IRA disappears or the nursing home injures your loved one, you can't take the wrongdoer to court where a jury of your peers will decide responsibility. Instead, you'll likely find your case before an arbitrator who's in the broker's or nursing home's pocket.

But the use of forced arbitration in the consumer space has become even more notorious of late. Above, I mentioned signing up for an app. I did so with a specific scenario in mind. More and more, companies are arguing that by signing up for their app that includes a forced-arbitration clause, you agree to arbitrate "any dispute arising under your relationship" with that company.

This means, for instance, if you signed up for a theme park's streaming service app and you died from an allergic reaction suffered at a restaurant at that theme park, your spouse can't sue because *you* agreed to arbitrate any disputes arising out of your relationship with the company, never mind that your app sign-up involved streaming services and not attendance at the theme park much less lunch at the restaurant.

Or if you signed up for a product-delivery service's app related to its music service and a truck delivering this company's product to someone else ran a red light and injured you, you can't sue because, again (and even more egregiously), in your contract relating to your *music service*, you agreed to arbitrate any—meaning *any*, no matter how attenuated—disputes arising out of your relationship with the company.

These are the sorts of cases that are out there, and they involve people just like us. Forced arbitration has proliferated to cover more and more scenarios that we as consumers would never expect. Just ask the couple whose rideshare driver ran a red light, nearly killing them. The judge dismissed their case in favor of forced-arbitration because their daughter had signed up for the company's food-delivery service using her mom's phone. In arbitration, the couple is sure to get only a sliver of what they require for their medical bills, lost wages, and pain and suffering due to the driver's clear negligence.

(See Appendix A for more information.)

2. Forced arbitration is radically different from court.

I've discussed the bought-and-paid-for nature of forced arbitration, but that's not where the unfairness ends.

Believe it or not, arbitrators aren't required to consider the law and legal precedent when making their decisions. Instead, they do their work in a black box, with no oversight or accountability. Worse still, whereas in court, you can appeal a judge's or jury's decision, you can't appeal an arbitrator's decision to confirm that they got it right. Instead, there's absolutely no public review of an arbitrator's decision, and you're required to keep it confidential.

And as I said, forced arbitration is often more expensive than taking a case to court. Though arbitration filing fees in consumer cases typically will be about $1,000, businesses may face even higher fees depending on the claim amount and the arbitration provider. For large claims, these fees can reach several thousand dollars. Also, these fees are usually nonrefundable and are due when filing the arbitration demand. When considering filing fees in court are around $300 to $400, many victims directed into arbitration are forced to get off on the wrong foot.

But perhaps worst of all, some forced-arbitration clauses include a "loser pays" provision. This means just what you think: If you arbitrate and lose, you're responsible for the company's expenses and attorneys' fees. Under the US justice system's American rule, the opposing sides in a lawsuit must pay their own attorneys' fees, regardless of who wins the case. The rationale of the rule is that a plaintiff should not be deterred from bringing a case to court for fear of prohibitive costs. Were it otherwise, nearly no one would be able to bring cases for their personal injuries, such as those that occur in auto accidents.

But the English rule provides that the party who loses pays the other side's legal costs. The English rule contrasts with the American rule, which is precisely why some companies include it in their forced-arbitration clauses. If anything would discourage someone from arbitrating, this clause is it.

Keep in mind that losing doesn't mean you deserved to. Often, it means the company has outspent and outgunned you because they have unlimited money and resources, including the aid of big, well-financed law firms. And if all that weren't bad enough, some forced-arbitration clauses require you to travel thousands of miles on your own dime to participate.

Simply put, people who've been harmed by negligence, defective products, and discrimination, who've been cheated out of wages, or who've been otherwise scammed should not be forced from public court into secret arbitration. They should have an honest choice of where they want to pursue their claim. But, sadly, they don't.

How Many Consumer Forced Arbitrations Actually Occur? Not Many.

According to the AAJ Report, from 2014 to 2018, the AAA and JAMs handled only about 30,000 consumer arbitrations—an average of 6,000 per year. To provide some context for that number, the AAA's total caseload is approximately 200,000 cases per year. Report at 9.

Class-action bans make forced-arbitration clauses even worse

I told you we'd deal with *Concepcion*'s class-action waiver language. Well, here it is.

Pouring your case into the black hole that is arbitration is bad enough. But there *is* that 7 percent or so chance of winning. In that case, how about filing a *class-action* arbitration, which is where one consumer has the potential to seek justice for thousands or perhaps millions of similarly situated victims? (We'll talk more about class actions in Chapter 21.) Even with a meager likelihood of success, this could help to even the scales of justice and leverage a settlement, right?

Wrong. *Concepcion* was a consumer class-action case. When the Supreme Court banished the Concepcions' claim to arbitration, the Court made sure to instruct that the Concepcions' arbitration needed to be on an individual—not classwide—basis. In this manner, the Court got the Concepcions (indeed, all consumers) coming and going: We must arbitrate our claims, and when we do, the arbitration must be individualized, meaning the stakes are far too small for any plaintiffs' lawyer (virtually all of whom are paid a contingency fee of one-third or so of any monetary recovery) to take it. In like manner, no company will be scared of an individual claim, meaning good luck encouraging a settlement.

Concepcion's one-two punch—forced arbitration and class-action ban (personally, I call it a *ban* because a *waiver* is the intentional relinquishment of a known right, and consumers *don't* know they're relinquishing their rights to class actions)—essentially eviscerated most small-dollar claims, thus, barring consumers from pursuing class-action lawsuits and leaving millions of consumers without a remedy for corporate wrongdoing.

Justice Breyer recognized this consequence in his dissent, where he observed that "[t]he *realistic* alternative to a class action is not 17 million individual suits, but zero individual suits, as only a lunatic or a fanatic sues for $30." *Concepcion*, 563 U.S. at 365 (Breyer, J., dissenting) (quoting *Carnegie v. Household Int'l, Inc.*, 376 F.3d 656, 661 (7th Cir. 2004) (emphasis in original)).

Simply put, forced-arbitration clauses and class-action bans hand companies a get-out-of-jail-free card for deceptive and fraudulent business practices, while consumers remain unable to vindicate their claims.

Despite all this, is there a way to get around forced-arbitration clauses?

This question returns us to my friends' Love Boat mess. As you saw, their arbitration clause was buttoned down nine ways to Sunday: A forced-arbitration requirement, a class-action ban, a forum-selection (or venue) clause requiring live attendance, an arbitrator selected by the cruise line, and half payment by my clients. Literally, it couldn't have been phrased worse. Yet I spent a lot of time writing that letter. And I got my friends their money back.

Remember, for these big companies, it's all about the money. That's why they lock you into forced-arbitration clauses in the first place. But often, as Justice Breyer remarked in *Concepcion*, consumer disputes are small-value claims. This means jurisdiction is almost always appropriate in small claims court in your home county. Granted, that doesn't mean the company can't move to stay your case and compel private arbitration, as occurred in *Concepcion*, which was a class action, not an individual claim. But nothing in the company's contract precludes you from initiating your case in small claims court—again, as occurred in *Concepcion*. Because remember, it's the *company's* burden to kick your case out of court if it wants to.

With this strategy in mind, I filed a complaint for my friends in small claims court in a Cleveland, Ohio, suburb—in particular, I filed my friends' claim in Cleveland Heights Municipal Court, which is located mere blocks from my friends' house. You'll remember, the Love Boat is headquartered in Boca Raton, Florida—not exactly down the street.[4]

This meant the cruise line's big-firm Miami lawyers would need to locate and hire expensive Cleveland lawyers (because clients with big-firm national counsel simply can't help hiring big-firm local counsel). And two sets of lawyers would mean two law firms (likely including a partner and an associate at each) working the case at excessively high rates, often with the associate doing all the work and the partner spending considerable time reviewing it before often doing the work again.

In addition to these start-up costs, if the big firmers wanted to kick the case to arbitration, that would mean a long and expensive process where the firms would research and write at least two court submissions—an opening memorandum (called a *brief*) and a closing brief—seeking a stay and transfer of the claim to forced arbitration, all over a $5,000 claim.

Considering what would easily cost the cruise line $20,000 before our case even set sail, about two weeks after I filed my clients' small claim and served their complaint on the Love

---

4 You'll also remember Justice Breyer's observation that nobody files small-value claims. That's often the case when the values are *really* small. But my friends' claim, while small, was still modest, unlike what Justice Breyer's observation contemplated. Because of that, their claim was worth pursuing.

Boat, I received a call from the cruise line's *in-house* counsel. I emphasize *in-house* to amplify how concerned about costs my filing made the cruise line. In-house counsel is on the company's payroll, meaning the company wasn't paying for this lawyer's involvement.

The in-house lawyer tried to posture a bit, suggesting that our case would never survive in small claims and would certainly end up in arbitration. I said maybe she was right, but I noted this process would be far from smooth sailing. Not only would the company require expensive local counsel, but also it would spend a ton of money to compel arbitration as compared to paying 100 percent of our small claim's value.

Added to all this was the abundantly nonlegal fact that I lived only minutes from the courthouse, whereas the in-house lawyer lived in Fort Lauderdale. I emphasized the degree to which I frequented the courthouse and knew the judge (and there's only one in that courthouse), laying it on thick and allowing my opponent to draw the appropriate inferences. For as they say, a good lawyer knows the law, but a *great* lawyer knows the judge.

By the time our conversation finished, the company agreed to write my clients a check for the full $5,000—an amount they would never have seen in an arbitration whose cost and inconvenience would have outstripped their claim's best-day value.

Of course, the Love Boat required my clients to sign a waiver and release indicating this sum resolved all disputes. But waivers and releases of settled claims are standard issue when settling legal disputes. You just need to make sure they're not overbroad—as in releasing *future* claims. This release was just fine.

You'll see I started with a letter (as I'm apt to do). After my letter sank, I followed it with a complaint. Sometimes, a letter will work (because the company doesn't want to live with the risk that you might sue); sometimes it won't (because the company calls your bluff, which the cruise line did). That's why I battened down the hatches and filed my complaint. Of course, if you want to cast off with a complaint, that's certainly your prerogative, though some small claims courts require an attempt at presuit resolution (as we'll discuss in Chapter 20), which I did.

As we've discussed, if you write a letter, state your case respectfully, include any necessary documentation, and make a reasonable ask. No hyperbole and no table pounding. The offending company's lawyers have seen it all, and they'll evaluate your letter emotionlessly. But your letter needs teeth. It's up to you to find the balance that works best for you.

My point is that even with forced-arbitration clauses, sometimes *you're* in the driver's seat. It's the company's job to raise arbitration, not yours. Often, they won't because it's easier and cheaper to simply pay you than to lawyer up. And in this manner, you might just end up beating big business at its own game.

Chapter 12
Fighting back against online offenses: defamation, doxing, and invasion of privacy

These days, perhaps the most perilous landscape to navigate—for yourself *and* your kids—is the Internet. And I'm not talking about the way the social media platforms infect our kids. I'm talking about a much more personal concern. I'm also not talking about a danger that could befall us via someone else's misbehavior. I'm talking about a danger to ourselves that *we* cause because *we* don't know the contours and limitations of what's legal and illegal online.

If *ever* an ounce of prevention were worth a hundred pounds of cure, it's in the online realm. If you don't believe me, just ask Amber Heard. No doubt she didn't know what was and wasn't okay to say online. Her lack of legal awareness ended up costing her a $15 million verdict—plus astronomical attorneys' fees. We'll unpack Heard's unfortunate and preventable misstep more in a bit.

Whether you like it or not, everyone is subject to getting sued, and the online frontier has opened limitless additional ways for that to happen. The brasher, more visible, and unaccountable a keyboard warrior you are, the more you expose yourself to litigation.

Considering this risk, who'd want to traverse this dangerous landscape with no understanding of the basic rules necessary to steer clear of trouble? Truth is, most people. Thoughtlessly surfing the Internet isn't much different than having no understanding of the traffic rules yet taking the wheel of a rickety old car with no seat belts or airbags and gunning it through Times Square. You'd have to be nuts to be that reckless, right? But people don't act much differently when it comes to their online behavior.

And when bad luck catches up to you (as it did to Amber Heard), the next important question is who pays the settlement or verdict? Is this amount self-pay, or does insurance cover it? If the latter, what type of coverage are we talking about? We'll unpack this important question in a bit, too.

Plus, we all know that kids post stupid things online, right? What happens when your minor child defames someone? Is their bad decision ascribable to you? If so, now we're talking about another person whose behavior requires supervision.

So just what types of lawsuits could reckless online conduct expose you to? To my mind, the main categories are expensive claims for defamation, doxing, and invasion of privacy (or video voyeurism). So let's dig in.

The dangerous particulars of online defamation

Of late, massive defamation suits have rocked the media landscape. Because of how hot the political discourse has become, the stakes invoked by defamation lawsuits, which always have a significant online component, as that's the way the actor's defamatory content proliferates, have exploded. In the past, a defamation lawsuit would have sought $1 million to $5 million, but now, these same claims often allege damages ranging anywhere from $10 million to $100 million.

Everything is so political these days, people often run to the courthouse to get their pound of flesh from those whose opinions they simply disagree with. And because defamation claims don't include caps on reputational harm the way caps limit personal injury damages, the sky can be the limit when you combine saying the allegedly wrong thing with a runaway jury.

But before digging into the consequences of defamation, it's necessary to describe precisely what defamation is. Defamation can take two forms, only one of which is susceptible to generation online.

Libel is the first form of defamation. Libel is a civil claim that protects someone's personal reputation against false and defamatory statements. A defamatory statement is one that seriously lowers a person's reputation by exposing them to hatred, shame, contempt, ridicule, aversion, and the like.

Slander is the other form of defamation. Slander is the act of making a false statement about someone to damage their reputation. Examples of slander are falsely accusing someone of a crime, falsely claiming someone has a disease, and falsely claiming someone is unable to do their job.

If libel and slander sound similar, it's because they are. The difference between these claims doesn't lie in what they pertain to; it lies in the way the alleged defamer communicated the defamatory statement. Libelous statements occur in writing, while slanderous statements occur orally.

Here's how I keep the two terms straight. Libel begins with an *L*, as in "literature," meaning the libelous statement must occur in writing. Slander begins with an *S*, as in "say," meaning you have to speak a slanderous statement. Because we're dealing with online issues, the defamation we'll be examining is libel, not slander.

1. If we're talking about defamation, it's essential to know a thing or two about the First Amendment.

Now that we have a little law under our belts, let's turn to the first place most people go when attempting to defend a libelous communication, whether online or elsewhere. That is, of course, the First Amendment. I often hear, "I have a First Amendment right to say whatever I'd like."

But not so fast. Not only are the First Amendment's application and sweep not ubiquitous, but its protections also come with limitations everyone should know, especially considering how inclined everyone is these days to share their opinions in writing via the Internet.

To begin, let's understand just what the First Amendment provides: "Congress shall make no law respecting an establishment or religion, or prohibiting the free exercise thereof; or abridging the freedom of speech, or of the press, or of the people to peaceably assemble, and to petition the Government for redress of grievances." First Amendment to the US Constitution (passed by Congress September 25, 1789; ratified December 15, 1791).

One of the ten amendments of the Bill of Rights, the First Amendment allows everyone residing in the United States the right to hear all sides of every issue and make their own judgments without governmental interference or limitations. This means we can speak as we'd like, publish what we choose, read what we want, view what we want, worship (or not worship) as we want, associate with whomever we choose, and gather to ask the government to change the law to address societal problems.

By its terms—"*Congress* shall make no law"—the First Amendment applies to the government, as well as to some actions taken by the government; it does *not* apply to private individuals or businesses—an important concept we'll address in a minute.

By establishing a framework that defines rights and responsibilities regarding free speech, expression, and belief, the First Amendment prevents public—not private—institutions from compromising people's freedoms. In this manner, Supreme Court Justice Louis Brandeis famously encouraged people living in the United States to resolve their differences in values and belief by resorting to "more speech, not enforced silence." *Whitney v. California*, 274 U.S. 357, 377 (1927).

Now, if the First Amendment is found in the US Constitution and not the various states' constitutions, how does it apply to the states? It applies to states because of the Fourteenth Amendment's Due Process Clause. The Supreme Court has interpreted this clause to mean states cannot deprive people of "liberty" without due process of law. *Gitlow v. New York*, 268 U.S. 652, 664 (1925).

This interpretation effectively incorporated most rights from the Bill of Rights, including the First Amendment, to apply to state governments. Therefore, criticism of the federal and state governments, political dissatisfaction with them, and advocacy of unpopular ideas nearly always gain First Amendment protection.

2. The First Amendment does not provide limitless protection, and in some instances, it doesn't provide protection at all.

The First Amendment does *not* provide limitless protection to people expressing ideas adverse to the federal and state governments. The Supreme Court has delineated several narrow categories of speech that the First Amendment doesn't protect.

Take, for instance, the expression, "You can't yell fire in a crowded theater." We've all heard it, right? This phrase implicates the limitations of the First Amendment. Because although the First Amendment prevents only the government from controlling our speech, often people believe the First Amendment protects *all* speech, which it doesn't.

> Now for a little Supreme Court inside baseball: The crowded-theater quote is attributed to U.S. Supreme Court Justice Oliver Wendell, who penned the Supreme Court's majority opinion in *Schenck v. United States,* 249 U.S. 47 (1919). But he didn't actually write the quote people think he did. Instead, he wrote, "[t]he most stringent protection of free speech would not protect a man in falsely shouting fire in a theatre and causing a panic." *Id.* at 52.

Notably, *Schenck* wasn't a First Amendment case. It involved the Espionage Act, and Justice Holmes's remark had nothing to do with the subject of the lawsuit. Instead, he expressed his crowded-theater idea as an analogy to illustrate that the First Amendment isn't absolute. Such language is called *dictum* (or *obiter dictum*) and is ancillary to the opinion in which it appears. It has no binding authority as it doesn't involve the facts of the case.

Accordingly, although the crowded-theater phrase is a popular way to demonstrate that the First Amendment has limitations, it's simply not the law that you can't yell fire in a crowded theater—a conclusion further validated when considering that the Supreme Court largely overturned *Schenck* fifty years later in *Brandenburg v. Ohio*, 395 U.S. 444 (1969).

Here are some types of speech the First Amendment doesn't protect:

- **Incitement to violence.** In *Brandenburg v. Ohio*, 395 U.S. 444 (1969), the Supreme Court held that the First Amendment protects advocating the use of force or lawbreaking "except where such advocacy is directed to inciting or producing imminent lawless action and is likely to incite or produce such action." *Id.* at 447. *Brandenberg's* "imminent lawless action" test provides a framework for balancing free speech rights with the government's interest in maintaining order and preventing violence.

- **Obscenity.** For material to be obscene, it must meet the standard set out by the Supreme Court in *Miller v. California*, 413 U.S. 15 (1973). The material, considered as a whole must "appeal to the prurient interest in sex," *id.* at 24 (as judged by contemporary community standards), depict or describe specifically defined sexual conduct in "a patently offensive way [and] lack[ ] serious literary, artistic, political, or scientific value." *Id.* That said, not all sexually explicit material is obscene.
- **Child sexual abuse material.** In *New York v. Ferber*, 458 U.S. 747 (1982), the Supreme Court recognized child pornography as a category of unprotected speech separate from obscenity. The Court reasoned that the advertising and sale of such materials are an integral part of their production. The Court explained that this category of unprotected speech involves materials that "visually depict sexual conduct by children below a specified age." *Id.* at 764. (The Court hasn't decided the First Amendment status of images altered by AI that depict identifiable minors, but I'm sure a decision will come before long.)
- **Defamation.** Defamation (our topic) involves false statements of fact about a person conveyed in writing (libel) or verbally (slander). Although defamatory statements are unprotected speech, the Supreme Court recognizes limits to this lack of protection. For instance, where an allegedly defamatory statement concerns a public official or figure, the person alleging defamation

must prove the speaker acted with "actual malice"—that is, knowledge that their statement was false or in reckless disregard of its truth or falsity.

- **Fighting words.** In *Chaplinsky v. New Hampshire*, 315 U.S. 568 (1942), the Supreme Court held that the First Amendment does not protect "fighting words, meaning words "likely to provoke the average person to retaliation, and thereby cause a breach of the peace." *Id.* at 574. But more recently, the Court tempered its ruling, stating that "speech cannot be restricted simply because it is upsetting or arouses contempt[, because i]f there is a bedrock principle underlying the First Amendment, it is that the government may not prohibit the expression of an idea simply because society finds the idea itself offensive or disagreeable." *Snyder v. Phelps*, 562 U.S. 443, 458 (2011).
- **True threats.** True threats (as distinguished from political hyperbole) occur when the speaker "means to communicate a serious expression of an intent to commit an act of unlawful violence to a particular individual or group of individuals." *Virginia v. Black*, 538 U.S. 343, 359 (2003). To qualify as unprotected speech, the speaker must have "consciously disregarded a substantial risk that [their] communications would be viewed as threatening violence." *Counterman v. Colorado*, 600 U.S. 66, 108 (2023).
- **Speech integral to criminal conduct.** The First Amendment affords no protection to speech "used as an integral part of conduct in violation of a valid criminal statute." *Giboney v. Empire Storage & Ice Co.*, 336 U.S. 490, 498 (1949). The Supreme Court has cited this rule as a reason why the government may prohibit

inchoate (or not fully formed) offenses such as conspiracy or solicitation to commit a crime.

- **Fraud.** Although the First Amendment does not categorically except false or misleading speech, certain types of fraudulent remarks fall outside of its protection. The government can pursue a false advertising claim against speakers who knowingly make factual misrepresentations to obtain money or another material benefit (such as employment). Also, proscriptions against perjury—knowingly giving false testimony under oath—are constitutional.

Finally, and separate from these exceptions, the First Amendment does *not* prevent restrictions on speech imposed by private individuals and companies. This is why social media providers and your employer can implement rules for what you can and can't say on their platforms or at your workplace. This is also why public universities must provide protesting students with greater latitude than private universities that aren't subject to the First Amendment's requirement, though many private universities, as bastions of learning, adopt the First Amendment's standards.

So when you say, "I have a First Amendment right to say whatever I'd like," you actually don't. You only have an unfettered right to say what you want so long as your speech doesn't trigger one of the unprotected categories and you're speaking in a public—not private—place.

3. But if the First Amendment has all these limitations (and in a private setting doesn't apply at all), how is it that the press seems able to publish whatever it wants?

I often hear, "If the press can print (or post) controversial content, why can't I?" This uninformed comparison invokes and is shaped and limited by the Supreme Court's uniquely famous case, *New York Times v. Sullivan*, 376 U.S. 254 (1964).

Sullivan established landmark precedent for freedom of speech protections for the press, not for individuals. The case involved a libel lawsuit brought by Montgomery, Alabama, police commissioner L.B. Sullivan against *The New York Times* involving a full-page ad that criticized southern officials for violating the rights of African Americans. Because the ad contained some factual inaccuracies, Sullivan argued it damaged his reputation.

The Supreme Court unanimously ruled for *The New York Times*. It established the "actual malice" rule that limits libel lawsuits to cases where the speaker acted with "reckless disregard" for the truth. (Did you notice I mentioned actual malice in the bullet point on defamation? This is what I was talking about.) The ruling also established that the First Amendment protects the right to publish statements about public officials, even if libelous, to encourage debate about public affairs.

This ruling is the Supreme Court's most famous libel decision and is considered one of the Court's greatest First Amendment decisions. It constitutionalized libel law and arguably saved the civil rights movement. But it's essential to recognize the limitations of this decision. It extended First Amendment protection to the press—not to individuals—when writing about government officials, not private citizens. Simply put, this means you may *not* take refuge in *New York Times Co. v. Sullivan* when defending an online defamation claim.

4. How does all this apply to my online content?

I laid out all this First Amendment material because (1) it's important to know, because all Americans deserve a baseline knowledge of the First Amendment's contours, application, and limitations, and (2) your knowledge of the First Amendment should inform what you can and can't say online and to whom. Most notably, you should now appreciate that you cannot blithely defend your online behavior against a private citizen by claiming your First Amendment right.

Consistent with all this, let's next consider what some high-profile people and companies thought was okay to say online and where their lack of legal awareness got them.

> **Dominion Voting Systems' defamation case against Fox News.** In April 2023, and only minutes before opening statements, Dominion settled its defamation against Fox for $787.5 million. Dominion's lawsuit alleged Fox and its anchors repeatedly and knowingly broadcast false information that Dominion participated in defrauding President Trump of reelection in 2020.
>
> **Sandy Hook families' defamation cases against Alex Jones.** In August 2022, a Texas jury ordered Alex Jones, host of *Infowars*, to pay the family of a Sandy Hook victim $4.1 million in compensatory damages and a whopping $45.2 million in punitive damages. The verdict derived from Jones's repeated contention that the

2021 tragedy was a false-flag operation by gun control advocates.

Two months later, a Connecticut jury awarded a first responder and the families of eight Sandy Hook victims $965 million in their defamation lawsuit against Jones. (See? Defamation damages have no caps.) The judge added another $473 million in punitive damages the next month.

E. Jean Carroll's defamation suit against Donald Trump. In May 2023, a New York City jury found Trump liable for defaming Carroll when he publicly denied her allegations that he'd sexually assaulted her in a department store dressing room in 1993. He insisted she "was totally lying." The jury awarded Carroll $5 million in damages.

Sarah Palin's defamation case against *The New York Times*. This example considers alleged defamation from the other end, meaning where the plaintiff—here, former Alaska governor Sarah Palin—lost. In February 2022, a New York City jury ruled that *The New York Times* did *not* defame Palin in an editorial that wrongly linked her campaign rhetoric to a 2022 mass shooting in Arizona, which the *Times* corrected in print the next day.

You'll remember from a few paragraphs above that the press has an extra level of protection against defamation claims, with the outlet needing to have made the alleged defamatory statement with actual malice—a level of scrutiny *not* provided to the rest of us. For this reason, the judge rejected Palin's request for a new trial,

> explaining that though the *Times* made mistakes, Palin's lawyers "could not in the end introduce even a speck of such evidence" that the *Times*' mistakes were motivated by actual malice. *Palin v. N.Y. Times Co.*, 604 F. Supp. 3d 208, 224 (S.D.N.Y. 2022).

These cases demonstrate that no one—no matter how high profile—is immune from a defamation lawsuit and the (more often than not) crippling damages associated with losing, which is more likely when you're not the press.

5. The law of unintended consequences: Johnny Depp v. Amber Heard

I know few of us own voting system companies or have served as a US president or governor. So to really drive home the way online overreach can affect people like us, let's return to *Johnny Depp v. Amber Heard*, as promised. This case is easily one of the most relatable, recognizable, and high-profile defamation lawsuits in years. And this *wasn't* a domestic violence case; it was a defamation case with an online component in that the op-ed Heard posted appeared online as everything does these days.

In 2019, Depp sued Heard for defamation after she wrote a 2018 op-ed in *The Washington Post*, alleging she was a victim of domestic abuse. Though her op-ed didn't mention Depp by name, the clear implication was that she was referring to him. He claimed $50 million in damages.

Depp's complaint claimed that Heard's op-ed damaged his reputation and career when explaining that she spoke up against "sexual violence" and "faced our culture's wrath," adding that "two years ago, [she] became a public figure representing domestic abuse [and] felt the full force of our culture's wrath for women who speak out[, and she] had the rare vantage point of seeing, in real time, how institutions protect men accused of abuse."[5] Though her op-ed was only 762 words, those few words had astronomical legal implications.

For Heard's part, and as a defensive (if not optical) measure, she filed a $100 million counterclaim (meaning her own lawsuit) against Depp, accusing him of defamation after his lawyer called her abuse claims a "hoax."

After years of expensive discovery (fact-finding conducted by the lawyers), the case went to trial in Fairfax, Virginia. (Depp filed his case there because *The Washington Post*'s online edition is published through servers in Fairfax County, Virginia; plus, Virginia defamation law favored Depp.)

The jury ruled for Depp on his three defamation claims and for Heard on one of her counterclaims. As a result, the jury awarded Depp $10 million in compensatory damages. The jury also awarded Depp $5 million in punitive damages, which the court reduced to $350,000 under Virginia state law, capping punitive damages. The jury awarded Heard $2 million in compensatory damages. On balance, Depp won.

And though on appeal, Depp and Heard settled their dispute with Heard paying $1 million to Depp, which he donated to five charities, there's no denying that this was a big-time out-of-pocket spend for Heard that she could have avoided had she known what constituted defamation.

Now it's time to get granular—to describe what not to do if you want to avoid ending up in the same pinch as Amber

[5] Amber Heard, "Amber Heard: I spoke up against sexual violence—and faced our culture's wrath. That has to change," *The Washington Post*, December 18, 2018, https://www.washingtonpost.com/opinions/ive-seen-how-institutions-protect-men-accused-of-abuse-heres-what-we-can-do/2018/12/18/71fd876a-02ed-11e9-b5df-5d3874f1ac36_story.html.

Heard. Earlier in this chapter, I described libel generally, but it's time to break it down into its specific elements. A legal claim's "elements" are the facts someone needs to prove to win a claim against you—in Johnny Depp's case, a claim for online libel or defamation. Put another way, a legal claim's elements are the facts you don't want to exist, meaning you don't want to have committed these facts because if you did, you'd likely lose.

So what facts did Depp prove that supported the jury's massive verdict against Heard? The answer lies in the special verdict form that the jury completed at the close of both sides' evidence.

The special verdict form asked the jury whether the following online statements Heard made satisfied the elements of defamation, meaning they were defamatory:

> "I spoke up against sexual violence—and faced our culture's wrath. That has to change."
>
> "Then two years ago, I became a public figure representing domestic abuse, and I felt the full force of our culture's wrath for women who speak out."
>
> "I had the rare vantage point of seeing, in real-time, how institutions protect men accused of abuse."

For these statements to have defamed Depp, the jury needed to conclude that they satisfied the following elements that constitute defamation under Virginia law:

1. "Did you find that Mr. Depp has proven the [following] elements of defamation?"
2. "The statement was made or published by Ms. Heard?"

3. "The statement was about Mr. Depp?"
4. "The statement ha[d] a defamatory implication about Mr. Depp?"
5. "The defamatory implication was designed and intended by Ms. Heard?"
6. "Due to circumstances surrounding the publication of the statement, it conveyed a defamatory implication to someone who saw it other than Mr. Depp."
7. "If you answered 'YES' to each subpart..., answer the following question: Do you find that Mr. Depp has proven by clear and convincing evidence that Ms. Heard acted with actual malice?"

Because the jury answered "yes" to all these questions, it awarded Depp $10 million in compensatory damages—to compensate him for the harm Heard's online defamation caused him—and $5 million in punitive damages that were intended to punish Heard for what the jury believed was egregious misconduct. (That was the actual malice part.)

As it concerned Heard's counterclaim for defamation against Depp's lawyer for calling her claim a hoax, the jury answered these same questions in the affirmative and awarded her $2 million in compensatory damages and $0 in punitive damages.

Looking at the special verdict form (see Appendix B), you can see how the lawyers boiled down the elements of a defamation claim under Virginia law into understandable soundbites that the jury could process and answer as Depp's lawyers wanted.

With this information in mind, think about things *you've* posted online, likely through X, TikTok, Facebook, or Instagram. Have *you* ever posted something online about someone that was false and so negative as to arguably be defamatory? When you did this, did you mean to insult or defame that person, perhaps because you were arguing politics, gay rights, gun violence, or the like, and they really pissed you off? And in this manner, did you post what you did with actual malice, meaning an intent to be spiteful or wicked, thinking, "That'll really show 'em!"

If you did these things in the context of a post—even a single post—you're susceptible to a lawsuit for defamation no different than Amber Heard was to Johnny Depp. That you *didn't* mean it or you *didn't* act maliciously is of no moment. For in the civil justice system, it doesn't matter what you believe; it only matters what you can prove. And to prove your defense means being in the soup—mired in litigation, years of legal filings, document discovery, depositions, hearings, and of course, expensive lawyers.

I'm guessing many of you didn't know what lurked behind the online defamation curtain—how easy it is to step into a dangerous space. With this insight, you also now know what someone can't say about *you*. In this manner, as Johnny Depp did, you have the legal awareness to know that you can pursue a defamation claim against someone whose behavior checks all the preceding boxes.

The dangers of doxing

"Doxing is a type of online harassment in which a person publishes someone's personal identifying information online without that person's consent." *Stiles v. Nelson*, No. CV-21-00533, 2022 U.S. Dist. LEXIS 6992, at *2 n.2 (D. Ariz. Jan. 13, 2022). Described slightly differently, doxing is also the "use of the Internet to search for and publish identifying information about a particular individual, typically with malicious intent." *Friends of Animals v. Bernhardt*, 15 F.4th 1254, 1277 n.3 (10th

Cir. 2021). However you slice it, courts considering doxing claims agree that doxing is an action one party maliciously takes against another.

Perhaps the most well-known incident of doxing involved YouTuber, actor, and boxer Jake Paul, where he filmed rapper Post Malone at his home without Malone's permission. In a video Paul would later delete, he delivers, unannounced, merchandise to Malone's home from Team 10, Paul's social-media-influencer brand.[6]

The video failed to blur Malone's neighborhood, the front of his house, or his front door—the type of data that would allow people to discover Malone's home address. But as they say, you can't put the toothpaste back in the (You)tube. Once the video was posted, the damage was already done. Indeed, one viewer claimed to have discovered Malone's address in only fifteen minutes.[7]

But California is different from most places in that scores of celebrities live there, especially in Los Angeles. So as you'd expect, California's electronic-eavesdropping laws provide extra protection against privacy invasion:

> A person who, intentionally and without the consent of all parties to a confidential communication, uses an electronic amplifying or recording device to eavesdrop upon or record

---

6 Toxic Productions, "Jake Paul Goes to Post Malone's House and Exposes Address," YouTube, July 22, 2017, 2 min., 26 sec. (redacted), https://www.youtube.com/watch?v=zKDtyG5tiq0 (no longer posted).

7 Perry470, "To Jake Paul's Defenders, I found Post Malone's Home Within 15 Minutes Using Jake's Already-Blurred Video," Reddit: r/h3h3productions, July 25, 2017, https://www.reddit.com/r/h3h3productions/comments/6pdyof/to_jake_pauls_defenders_i_found_post_malones_home/?rdt=52729 (no longer posted).

> the confidential communication, whether the communication is carried on among the parties in the presence of another or by means of a telegraph, telephone, or other device, except a radio, shall be punished by a fine not exceeding two thousand five hundred dollars ($2,500) per violation, or imprisonment in a county jail not exceeding one year, or in the state prison, or by both that fine and imprisonment.
>
> California Penal Code § 632.

Eavesdropping, as proscribed by section 632, can be prosecuted as a misdemeanor, which carries a maximum one-year prison sentence, or a felony, which carries a maximum three-year sentence. *See* California Penal Code 1170(h)(1) ("[F]elony punishable pursuant to this subdivision where the term is not specified in the underlying offense shall be punishable by a term of imprisonment in a county jail for 16 months, or two or three years.").

Importantly, California is a "two-party consent" state. This means all parties to a telephone call or conversation must give their consent before someone can record it. Most states are one-party consent states, meaning for a recording to be legal, only one party (obviously, the recording party) needs to know it's being recorded. *See* Chapter 7.

From the video, it appears Malone didn't know Paul was recording him. Paul never produced a camera, and Malone never looked into or acknowledged one. And though, after a few moments, Paul quipped, "Can we vlog or no?" to which Malone, while running around looking for his pants, snapped, "Sure, let's do it," Paul never said anything to Malone about

Paul's friend waiting in the car with blacked-out windows, recording on a camera with a telephoto lens. Once back in the car, Paul even asked this friend whether he'd gotten "the sniper shot."

Based on these facts, California criminal law, which it seems Paul didn't know about, would support a criminal case. But if that weren't bad enough, his conduct also violated California civil invasion-of-privacy law. (Violations of criminal law result in fines and jail time; violations of civil law result in money damages.)

Paul's behavior triggered two types of civil invasion of privacy under California law:

> **Public disclosure of private facts.** Remember, to determine whether someone has a civil claim against you (as Johnny Depp had against Amber Heard), we need to examine the elements of the claim alleged. The elements of a claim for public disclosure of private facts in California are (1) public disclosure of a (2) private fact that (3) would be offensive and objectionable to a reasonable person and that (4) is not a legitimate public concern or interest. *Catsouras v. Dep't of Cal. Highway Patrol*, 181 Cal. App. 4th 856, 903 (2010).
>
> In determining what is a matter of legitimate public interest, the courts take account of "the customs and conventions of the community[,] and...what is proper becomes a matter of the community mores." *Virgil v. Time, Inc.*, 527 F.2d 1122, 1129 (9th Cir. 1975) (quoting

Restatement (Second) of Torts § 652D comment f (1975)). Courts draw the line where "the publicity ceases to be the giving of information to which the public is entitled[] and becomes a morbid and sensational prying into private lives for its own sake, with which a reasonable member of the public, with decent standards, would say that he had no concern." *Id.*

Channeled through these elements and the courts' application of them, it's easy to conclude that Paul exposed himself to civil liability for publicly disclosing Malone's address. He disclosed a private fact reasonably offensive and objectionable to Malone that was not of legitimate public concern or interest. And let's not forget Paul's one-party recording that triggered California's *criminal* statute.

Just as Amber Heard likely didn't know she was violating Virginia defamation law, Paul likely didn't know he was violating California defamation law. When considering the similarity among defamation laws nationwide, you now have an idea of what sort of online behavior could land you in trouble.

Intrusion into private matters. We know where to start; it's with the elements of an intrusion-into-private-matters claim under California law. The elements are (1) defendant's intentional intrusion, physical or otherwise (2) into plaintiff's private life, seclusion, or solitude that (3) would be highly objectionable to a reasonable person, and (4) it's the cause of an adverse effect on the plaintiff.

Delineating these elements can sometimes be elusive. So here's a case where the plaintiff satisfied them. It involved a man who'd suffered a heart attack, and a TV camera crew entered his home without his permission to film a story about paramedics and their life-saving techniques. The man died, and the TV station aired portions of the tape on the news when advertising a minidocumentary about the paramedics' work. *Miller v Nat'l Broad. Co.*, 187 Cal. App. 3d 1463 (1986).

The decedent's wife sued the station. The court ruled that she stated a cause of action for breach of privacy by intrusion because "reasonable people could regard the NBC camera crew's intrusion into [decedent's] bedroom at a time of vulnerability and confusion occasioned by his seizure as 'highly offensive' conduct, thus meeting the limitation on a privacy cause of action." *Id.* at 1484.

Against this precedent, and after analyzing the elements of Malone's intrusion into private matters claim, it's easy to conclude that Paul's behavior crossed the line, thus exposing him to civil liability and monetary damages. Paul

> took Malone's address from Fanjoy, the third-party provider through which Malone placed his clothing order. Then, Paul showed up without warning at Malone's home, identified his home, secretly filmed the entire interaction, including Malone in his underwear, and posted his handiwork online for his millions of followers. Posting his video on the Internet made a bad situation worse, especially when considering he published the video without Malone's knowledge.
>
> And if you think Fanjoy is blameless, think again. Fanjoy was also subject to privacy liability for failing to keep its customers' personal information private under California Civil Code section 1798.81.5(a)(1) ("It is the intent of the Legislature to ensure that personal information about California residents is protected. To that end, the purpose of this section is to encourage businesses that own, license, or maintain personal information about Californians to provide reasonable security for that information.").

So, again, think of the things you've said, likely on social media, perhaps in the heat of a battle about politics or social issues. If you go too far, including posting personal data about someone, you could be looking for trouble. Sure, Jake Paul was an extreme example, but online defamation needn't rise to that level. For instance, if you have a target who's highly sensitive to online privacy issues—perhaps because their privacy has been compromised before—it could be more likely they'd file a doxing claim against you even if you don't think you did anything that deserved it.

Invasion of privacy and the creepy practice of video voyeurism

To my mind, the grisliest and most offensive form of online misbehavior is video voyeurism. This means posting, for absolutely no good reason, videos of people (mostly women by men) in compromised states, whether of undress or in personal settings.

All states have laws criminalizing video voyeurism. Here's one state's robust statute defining the offense:

> (a) The following definitions apply throughout this section:
>
> (1) "Camera" means a camera, a video camera, a device that captures a digital image, or any other type of video recording device.
>
> (2) "Peep" means:
>
> (A) any looking of a clandestine, surreptitious, prying, or secretive nature; or
>
> (B) using a concealed camera with the intent of capturing an intimate image....
>
> (3) "Private area" means the naked or undergarment clad genitals, pubic area, or buttocks of an individual.

(b) A person:

(1) who knowingly or intentionally:

(A) peeps; or

(B) goes upon the land of another with the intent to peep; into an occupied dwelling of another person; or

(2) who knowingly or intentionally peeps in or into an area where an occupant of the area reasonably can be expected to disrobe or is actually expected to disrobe, including:

(A) restrooms;

(B) baths;

(C) showers; and

(D) dressing rooms;

without the consent of the other person, commits voyeurism, a Class B misdemeanor.

(c) However, the offense under subsection (b) is a Level 6 felony if:

(1) it is knowingly or intentionally committed by means of a camera; or

(2) the person who commits the offense has a prior unrelated conviction under this section.

(d) A person who:

(1) without the consent of the individual; and

(2) with intent to peep at the private area of an individual; peeps at the private area of an individual and records an image by means of a camera commits public voyeurism, a Class A misdemeanor.

(e) The offense under subsection (d) is a Level 6 felony if the person has a prior unrelated conviction under this section or if the person:

(1) publishes the image;

(2) makes the image available on the Internet; or

(3) transmits or disseminates the image to another person.

(f) It is a defense to a prosecution under subsection (d) that the individual deliberately exposed the individual's private area.

(g) A person who, with the intent to peep, operates an unmanned aerial vehicle in a manner that is intended to cause the unmanned aerial vehicle to enter the space above or surrounding another person's occupied dwelling for the purpose of capturing images, photographs, video recordings, or audio recordings of the other person while the other person is:

(1) within the other person's occupied dwelling; or

(2) on the land or premises:

(A) on which the other person's occupied dwelling is located; and

(B) in a location that is not visible from an area:

(i) open to the general public; or

(ii) where a member of the general public has the right to be; commits remote aerial voyeurism, a Class A misdemeanor.

Ind. Code Ann. § 35-45-4-5.

Video voyeurism is also a crime under federal law:

(a) Whoever, in the special maritime and territorial jurisdiction of the United States, has the intent to capture an image of a private area of an individual without their consent, and knowingly does so under circumstances in which the individual has a reasonable expectation of privacy, shall be fined under this title or imprisoned not more than one year, or both.

(b) In this section—

(1) the term "capture," with respect to an image, means to videotape, photograph, film, record by any means, or broadcast;

(2) the term "broadcast" means to electronically transmit a visual image with the intent that it be viewed by a person or persons;

(3) the term "a private area of the individual" means the naked or undergarment clad genitals, pubic area, buttocks, or female breast of that individual;

(4) the term "female breast" means any portion of the female breast below the top of the areola; and

(5) the term "under circumstances in which that individual has a reasonable expectation of privacy" means—

(A) circumstances in which a reasonable person would believe that he or she could disrobe in privacy, without being concerned that an image of a private area of the individual was being captured; or

(B) circumstances in which a reasonable person would believe that a private area of the individual would not be visible to the public, regardless of whether that person is in a public or private place.

(c) This section does not prohibit any lawful law enforcement, correctional, or intelligence activity.

18 U.S.C. § 1801.

While some states, like Connecticut, may not have specific voyeurism statutes, voyeurism in those states is still illegal and subject to prosecution under other statutes, such as trespass, disorderly conduct, or breach of the peace.

As you can see, state and federal governments take voyeurism seriously, and convictions can result in long-term consequences. Moreover, a video-voyeurism conviction can lead to being listed on a sex-offender registry.

But the consequences of video voyeurism don't stop with a criminal conviction. Often following (or contemporaneous with) criminal prosecution comes a civil claim, meaning the possibility of money damages owed to the victim.

The criminal and civil dimensions of online voyeurism made front-page headlines when an online voyeur victimized TV sportscaster Erin Andrews by videotaping her with his cell phone camera through a removed peephole during her stay at a Nashville Marriott at Vanderbilt University. The voyeur, Michael David Barrett, later posted the video online.

Barrett was found, arrested, and served two-and-a-half years in prison for interstate stalking. Also, Andrews sued him and the hotel's owner and operator. A civil jury ordered Barrett to pay Andrews $28 million and the hotel owner and operator about $26 million.

The basis for civil liability against Barrett is simple enough—he was the voyeur. But because he had no money, Andrews' lawyers needed to be creative. They argued that the hotel's owner and operator should have kept Barrett from finding out where Andrews was staying and from booking a room next to hers, from which he listened for when her shower started and stopped before recording. Her lawyers also argued the hotel should have alerted her that someone had asked to sleep next door.

From this example, you can see that the consequences of online voyeurism can extend beyond the voyeur. This is why, in addition to never engaging in such behavior yourself, you might have a duty to ensure that people in your sphere of influence don't either.

Building on the Erin Andrews case, here's another example of the risks associated with voyeurism—this one uniquely personal. I'm lead counsel in a video-voyeurism class-action lawsuit in California against a school district and one of its high school's former assistant football coaches. It turned out that for perhaps as many as six years, the coach spied on virtually every girl in the school by planting, in the girls' locker room and bathroom, one or more video cameras disguised as iPhone chargers.

During this time, he harvested almost 7,000 images of underage girls in various stages of undress or conducting personal business. Some images included girls' faces; some didn't. And none of the girls knew whether he posted the images online for others to see, even to this day.

I sued the coach for his behavior. But seeing as the coach, like Barrett, has no money (in addition to the fact that he's serving nine years in a California state prison for violating California's video-voyeurism laws), I also sued the school district, alleging its negligence in failing to implement a single protocol to ensure against (or at least minimize) the potential for video voyeurism—a practice that is well-known in educational circles, pervasive, and easy to detect.

And if you're thinking, "If a girl's face weren't caught on tape, what's the difference, including whether he posted the video?" The difference is not only that the coach's conduct was so patently offensive as to shock the conscience, but also, under California law (and perhaps in keeping with the offensiveness of such behavior), it's not necessary for someone's face to have been captured for civil liability to exist.

In *Hernandez v. Hillsides, Inc.*, 47 Cal. 4th 272 (2009), an employer placed a hidden camera in an office used by the plaintiffs. The employer "never viewed or recorded plaintiffs inside their office by means of the equipment he installed both there and in the storage room" or even attempted to. *Id.* at 293. In fact, he "took steps to avoid capturing them on camera and videotape." *Id.*

Based on the mere presence of the camera alone, the employees brought claims of negligence and invasion of privacy. *Id.* at 279. The defendants argued (as the school district did in my case) that the plaintiffs had no actionable claim for invasion of privacy "absent evidence [that the employer] targeted and either viewed or recorded plaintiffs as part of the surveillance scheme." *Id.* at 277.

But the California Supreme Court disagreed. Rejecting the argument and assessing the employees' privacy claims "under the rubric of both the common law and constitutional tests for establishing a privacy violation," *id.* at 288, the court distilled a test that "considered (1) the nature of any intrusion upon reasonable expectations of privacy, and (2) the offensiveness or seriousness of the intrusion, including any justification and other relevant interests." *Id.*

Applying this test, the court held that actual recording of a person is not required to satisfy the first element, *id.* at 294, adding "[f]ailure to capture or record the subject image is no defense" to "[o]ther statutes [that] authorize civil damages for certain invasions of privacy that involved physical trespass or other offensive conduct for the purpose of capturing a picture of someone engaged in personal or familial activities." *Id.* at

292. It was enough that the employer "install[ed] electronic equipment that gave it the *capacity* to secretly watch and record employee activities behind closed doors in an office to which the general public had limited access." *Id.* at 289–90 (emphasis added).

Considering this generous jurisprudence, I hope I'm able to make my negligence case stick against the school district for its failure to enlist protocols to detect and avoid the obvious youth-voyeurism epidemic, whether girls' faces were captured or not. After all, protocols exist concerning other devices, such as cell phones and laptops, and other behavior, such as bullying. When considering the number of girls to pass through the locker room and bathroom over six years, I'm seeking tens of millions of dollars in damages for these girls, many of whom were significantly affected by what they learned the coach did and their school district didn't.

So that's how criminal and civil liability can flow from the same dangerous act. Now that you know both consequences, I hope you'll agree it's a bad idea to engage in video voyeurism. After all, not only do voyeurs always get caught (because they don't suitably cover their tracks), but also the evidence is always there to hang the perpetrator. Indeed, preserving illegal images is the whole point of video voyeurism. But, again, as with the other noteworthy forms of online defamation, what's good is that trouble is completely avoidable. Indeed, and as my grandmother used to tell me, you can't get into trouble with your mouth—or in this case, your lens—shut.

In addition to suing a defamer, doxer, or voyeur, can you sue Google for hosting the offender's content?

So far, we've been discussing what not to do if you want to avoid getting sued for online behavior. This has involved the criminal and civil consequences of not knowing the law. Now, let's flip the script and say someone defames or violates *you* online, as Barrett did to Erin Andrews. Let's add that the violator (again, like Barrett) has no meaningful assets, but there *isn't* a deep pocket to go after, like the hotel or, in my case, a school district.

Let's also say the defamer's ugly message or video appeared all over your—and others'—search results. We all know that without a search engine to circulate the defamer's ugly content, no one could read or watch it. So what about suing Google for publishing this violative content? Can't you just do *that*?

The answer to that question is "no" because of Section 230 of the Communications Decency Act (CDA). The CDA is a law passed by Congress in 1996 to regulate the distribution of obscene and indecent content online. But robust as the CDA is, it has limitations. Section 230 immunizes interactive computer services like Google, Yahoo, and Bing from liability for third parties' actions.

The CDA states that "No provider or user of an interactive computer service should be treated as the publisher or speaker of any information provided by another information content provider." This language is often referred to as "the twenty-six words that created the Internet." And this stands to reason because if search engines were on the hook for posting other people's content, we'd have no Internet.

Sure, Section 230 contains a few exceptions, such as where Google *created* the content or if Google is contributorily liable for copyright or trademark infringement, but those situations rarely occur. The bottom line is that if someone defames you online, you can't sue Google. Taken from the other end, if you defame someone online, there's no Google backstop you can rely on your victim suing—you're likely going to be it. If you don't believe me, Google it.

Does your insurance cover you for lawsuits related to online behavior?

What if you're not intending to defame, yet you're politically and socially active online? We all know that with robust online activity comes the potential to rankle someone. Worse yet, many of us have gotten involved in races to the bottom, where the barbs fly fast and furiously. To make matters worse, all your smart-mouthed content is preserved electronically.

Despite your intentions simply to engage in online discourse, what if you get sued for online defamation by someone claiming your online behavior wasn't much different than Jake Paul's or Michael David Barrett's? (Proving you didn't intend to act with actual malice is a defense to a lawsuit, meaning you can only demonstrate it *after* a lawsuit is underway; this defense won't avoid a lawsuit.) And if you end up on the wrong end of a jury verdict, which, as I've demonstrated, can be astronomical, how in the world will you pay it?

A standard homeowners' insurance policy does not cover online defamation claims. You need to have "personal injury" coverage. Personal injury coverage is an optional endorsement on a standard homeowners' policy that provides protection for libel, slander, defamation of character, false arrest, malicious prosecution, and wrongful eviction.

The need for robust homeowners' coverage.

The first thing is to ensure that you have a homeowners' policy. If you do, you can purchase a personal injury endorsement (or rider) to add to your policy. This provides additional legal protection against defamation claims if committed in your home and if the defamation was unintentional. This means if you're at home and you fire off something online that's true yet offends someone and the subject sues you for defamation, your homeowners' coverage, via the personal injury rider, would likely protect you.

Though you might need personal injury coverage on your homeowners' policy, don't forget about personal liability coverage.

Personal liability coverage is different from your homeowners' policy's personal injury coverage. Before we dig deep into personal injury coverage and its application to online defamation claims, personal liability coverage deserves some attention.

Personal liability is a coverage included on your homeowners' or renters' policy that provides reimbursement for injuries caused to others on your property. It also covers damage to others' property on your property. So if someone slips on your kitchen floor, injures themselves, and shatters their expensive watch, your homeowners' policy's personal liability coverage would pay their personal injury and property damage claims. This would include medical bills, lost wages, pain and suffering, and, of course, a new watch. Plus, if your (by now, likely ex-) friend ends up suing you, this coverage would also pay for lawyers to defend you.

You'll notice the scenario I described in the preceding paragraph involved coverage for someone getting hurt on your property. What if you hurt someone outside your property? What if your daughter, while playing at a friend's house, accidentally hits a baseball through their neighbor's window, or your toddler son cuts off an elderly man walking in the mall, causing him to fall and injure himself? Your personal liability should cover these situations, too; although, you'll want to check your policy to be sure.

But personal liability coverage *doesn't* cover everything. Importantly, coverage would likely exclude intentional injury or property damage to another, injury or property damage to another person in your household, injury or property damages related to business activities (you'd need a commercial liability insurance policy for that), and damage to your car (you have auto insurance for that).

Don't forget about an umbrella policy

But wait—there's another important thing to add before returning to personal injury coverage. In addition to your homeowners' policy's personal liability coverage, you can further protect yourself by purchasing what is known as an umbrella liability policy. An umbrella provides additional coverage (at a higher premium, of course) for when extraordinarily unfortunate things happen in your home or on the road. In this manner, a multimillion-dollar umbrella policy would protect you if, heaven forbid, the person who slipped and fell in your home died or you killed someone with your car, because your normal liability limits would probably be insufficient to cover a settlement or verdict.

Now for that deep dive into personal injury coverage for online defamation.

Personal injury coverage is not automatically included in a homeowners' insurance policy. You'll have to pay for an endorsement or rider if you want it. This extra premium payment will get you not only coverage for a claim alleging libel, slander, defamation of character, false arrest, malicious prosecution, and wrongful eviction, but it will also get you coverage for legal counsel.

Importantly, personal injury coverage doesn't allow you to post anything you want about somebody. As with personal liability coverage, personal injury coverage has exclusions. As you've likely guessed by now, personal injury coverage doesn't cover you for knowingly using defamatory language. This means personal injury coverage doesn't cover you for acts where you knew the information was false or would violate someone else's rights—malice, as I discussed previously. Your online content needs to have been an innocent mistake.

So far, I've focused on defamation claims filed by individuals. But that's certainly not the universe of plaintiffs who could sue you. Lawyers, doctors, churches, synagogues, and small businesses are equally able to file lawsuits for online defamation resulting from cutting online remarks.

Think about it: A bad online review can affect a professional's or religious institution's reputation. If you're venting about a bad experience you've had with someone, you'd better have the facts to back it up. Because if the comments affect the entity's reputation or keep others from doing business with them, the business owner could fact check you—big time. And if they detect any way to even the scales by suing you, you'd best watch out.

But let's say your online content was true. As I've described, even if your remarks are true—and mindful that "truth is an absolute defense to defamation," *Ditzel v. Univ. of Med. & Dentistry of N.J.*, 962 F. Supp. 595, 605 (D.N.J. 1997)—that defense only becomes relevant in the context of a pending lawsuit. This means you can only prove this defense *after* you're already in court, which means you're spending money.

This is why—never mind what I think about a product or service I've purchased—I *never* post a bad (and sometimes permanent) online review. At best, you'll perhaps (though probably not) discourage someone from doing business with the company; at worst, you'll get sued. You tell me which is the smart choice.

In keeping with the vulnerability that online content poses, many employers have begun requesting potential employees' social media usernames and handles, so they can see how they can expect these prospects to conduct themselves away from work. This is another reason not to be a big shot or keyboard warrior from the privacy of your basement, which I hope I've demonstrated isn't so private after all.

So what's the bottom line when it comes to insurance coverage for online defamation? There's coverage for it (so long as your content is true, meaning it's actually *not* defamation, and it occurs in your home for nonbusiness reasons). But don't make the mistake of believing that personal liability coverage, which most people have with their homeowners' policy, is the same thing as personal injury coverage. If you think you need both, this is a discussion you should have with your insurance agent, though perhaps the better (and cheaper) approach would be simply to not risk defaming anyone online in the first place.

Where can you turn if you're sued for online defamation that occurred at your business instead of your home? That's where media liability coverage comes in.

Till this point, the discussion has centered on keyboard warriors popping off from home against individuals or companies. Now, let's say you own a business, and you don't like how your competitor's advertising or conduct is affecting your sales. So you decide to take matters into your own hands by skewering them or perhaps addressing their tactics on the Internet, whether through review sites or posting a dedicated webpage. Will your homeowners' coverage's personal injury endorsement cover you when your competitor sues you? Probably not.

What is media liability coverage, and how could it help?

If you're a business owner, when it comes to posting comments, making videos, writing articles, or producing advertisements, there's always the chance you'll rub a competitor (or a consumer) the wrong way. And these days, as we know, something like that can result in a defamation lawsuit.

One way to protect your business (and yourself) from this possibility is through media liability insurance. This coverage protects your company from third-party liability claims.

A deep dive into the specifics of media liability insurance to see how it might benefit your business.

Most small business owners are familiar with errors and omissions (E&O), workers' compensation, and commercial auto coverage but not so much with media liability coverage. The easiest way to explain media liability coverage is to think of it as a more specialized version of an E&O policy.

Like E&O coverage, media liability insurance protects your business from claims that you made a mistake while providing a professional service. But media liability coverage is different from E&O coverage in that its primary function is to provide protection related to media services. That means media liability coverage will generally extend to claims for defamation, invasion of privacy, and disparagement.

Media liability coverage has plenty of benefits. For instance, it could cover a competitor's defamation claim deriving from online disparagement of its competing product. Businesses that publish written or visual content would benefit from media liability coverage, such as:

- Photographers
- News broadcasters
- Bloggers
- Advertising agencies
- Social and digital media consultants
- Print and online newspaper and newsletter publishers
- Film producers
- Podcast hosts

If you operate in any of these areas, it might be worth talking to your insurance agent about media liability coverage.

What is the difference between media liability and general liability insurance?

Though you might think your business's commercial general liability (CGL) policy covers online defamation, that's not necessarily so. The main difference between a CGL policy and a media liability policy is that, while a CGL policy provides coverage for advertising injury, it often doesn't cover other media-related risks, such as libel and slander (i.e., online defamation), the risks of which are especially acute if you are involved in any form of advertising, broadcasting, or publishing.

Vicarious liability for your minor kids' online misconduct

Everyone's kids do dumb stuff. Heck, *I* did plenty of dumb stuff, from throwing a baseball through our neighbors' window to leaving my friend's back door open, letting out the cat.

But now, dumb stuff has a whole new playground—the Internet: the place where kids stupidly post ugly content about people, thinking they're too clever to be detected, though we adults know that's not true.

You see where this section is headed. What if it's not you who defames someone online, but your kid, who's in control of the keyboard, often from the seclusion of their bedroom or the recesses of your basement? What if your kid ends up on the receiving end of an online defamation lawsuit because they didn't know the contours and limitations of defamation liability—instructions described here that you didn't have a chance to share with them? Are *you* legally liable for what *they* did? You certainly could be. (All the more reason to share this chapter.)

Parental civil liability for kids is a form of "vicarious liability"—a legal principle that holds one party responsible for the actions of another party even though the other party is primarily responsible. (The Latin word vicarious means "substitute.") The most commonly recognized form of vicarious liability is *respondeat superior*—a legal doctrine that holds an employer liable for the actions of their employees when those actions occur within the course and scope of the employee's employment. (The term is Latin for "let the master answer.")

For our purposes, here's a common scenario: A minor child injures someone or damages their property, such as in my baseball and cat examples. Though the parent didn't commit the negligent act, vicarious liability would extend to the parent based on their supervision of their child (or lack thereof) and their child's conduct.

Rest assured, parental civil liability differs from parental criminal liability. Sometimes, the law identifies a parent's misconduct or behaviors as criminal acts, such as when parents of minor mass shooters are prosecuted for their failure to properly supervise their child or for providing their child with a semiautomatic weapon. Less extreme examples include contributing to the delinquency of a minor or endangering a child. The civil liability we'll discuss exposes a parent to monetary damages, whereas criminal liability exposes a parent to potential jail time and fines.

The age of majority is 18 in virtually all states. The age of majority affects a person's voting rights and ability to get married, own property, and join the military. When a child reaches the age of majority, they are legally considered an adult, and the rights and responsibilities of their parents transfer to them. Some of the upsides of this transfer are the new adult's ability to open a checking account or get a credit card, participate in a retirement savings account, or open other investment accounts.

One downside for young adults is that they are now responsible for their own "torts" or civil wrongs, including online defamation. This means that until your kid reaches the age of majority in your state, *you* are most likely responsible for their civil misbehaviors, including any monetary damages that could result from them.

Accordingly, states' parental responsibility laws hold parents financially responsible to varying degrees (some, including attorneys' fees) for damages caused by their minor children. Damages may stem from personal injury or property damage that the child causes.

This means you could be on the hook for your kid throwing the baseball through the neighbor's window or leaving the back door open. More seriously, you could be responsible for injuries and property damage stemming from your child's auto accident, or, yes, online defamation generated from their bedroom or your basement.

Once your child reaches the age of majority, they are no longer a minor, and you are no longer liable for their legal wrongs. A termination of parental rights also ends the legal parent-child obligation.

To be a bit more precise, state laws vary on the level of intent required to invoke parental liability. Some states require proof that your child committed willful acts or engaged in willful misconduct, such as vandalism, as opposed to carelessness, such as bumping into an elderly person at the mall. Other states may find you liable for the acts of your children without such intent.

State laws also vary regarding the types and amounts of damages available in a parental-liability lawsuit. Some states provide for only compensatory or actual damages, meaning money required to make the injured party whole (e.g., medical bills, lost wages, payment to repair damaged property) and cap the injured party's total damages. In other states, if you lose, the injured party could also recover attorneys' fees and the expenses necessary for them to pursue their lawsuit.

And while it's one thing to say *that* you might be responsible for your kid's online defamation, the bigger question is *why*—as in what's the legal theory or hook that makes this so? It's called "negligent supervision."

A parent is liable for their child's negligent acts if they know or have reason to know it's necessary to control their child yet fail to take reasonable actions to do so. This legal theory stems from the common law (meaning long-standing, judge-made) tort of negligence.

But liability for negligent supervision is not limited to parents. Grandparents, guardians, and others with custody and control of a child could also be liable for negligent supervision. Considering this broad exposure, it's extra essential to have a solid homeowners' policy, including umbrella coverage. See how these concepts blend together?

***

I'll end with a sad and personal story about all this. My daughter has a good friend from high school. They went off to college, where my daughter's friend majored in film studies. Part of her friend's film studies experience involved interning, and she found herself an internship with one of the best young producers in town. He worked her hard, but she didn't care. She wanted the maximum experience possible.

This producer had issues, which he projected onto my daughter's friend. Suddenly, my daughter's friend was apparently never on time, she never asked the right questions, and she always gave the wrong answers. But worst of all, when the producer messed up clients' projects, he always blamed my daughter's friend. He refused to take responsibility or ownership for anything that went wrong.

This unfair transferal started innocently enough, with modest blame for this and that. But the blame grew more frequent and more intense. Then the *real* problems began. The producer became concerned that the world would attribute his mistakes to him (as it should have). He needed to ensure that this didn't occur, so he began posting disparaging messages about my daughter's friend online.

His ugly messaging began by describing how my daughter's friend was holding his company back. Then, the messages grew uglier. While lauding his company's successes, he castigated her for screwing up when she hadn't and credited himself for overcoming her supposed interference.

Then, the comments started. People began to pile onto my daughter's friend. But the more she defended herself, the deeper the hole she dug. After all, who'd believe a lowly intern over a well-respected producer?

She didn't know what to do, so she didn't act against the producer, who finally fired her. But when she sought another intern job in town, no one would talk to her because she was damaged goods. In a small field, word travels fast, and she lost all hope.

Ultimately, feeling like there was nowhere to go, she dropped out of school and enrolled in a day program across the country. School is on hold, if she'll ever finish it. She didn't take swift action against her defamer because neither she nor her parents knew she could. They didn't know about online defamation law or the steps victims can take. If anything positive comes from this tragic story, let it be that this sort of thing doesn't happen to you or your kids.

Simply put, technology is evolving faster than our aptitude for it. Online tools are ubiquitous, accessible, and fraught with peril. Placing a cell phone in your kid's hands isn't much different than giving them the keys to your car. Why in the world would you do it without adequate information? Sit down with your child, emphasize the perils that this chapter identifies, and make sure neither they nor you get anywhere close to behavior that constitutes online defamation, doxing, or invasion of privacy.

Chapter 13
Your rights when robocallers try to scam you

Hardly a day goes by that I don't receive a robocall, whether offering me a vacation package, inquiring if I've been in an auto accident, or claiming the caller (though not even a person) is an officer with the Social Security Administration. The reason robocalls are at epidemic levels is that they make the robocallers money. And how? Because people still fall for them.

Robocalling and robotexting are big business. The scammers used to include robofaxing, remember? That's died down because pretty much only the medical profession uses fax machines these days due to the Health Insurance Portability and Accountability Act (HIPAA) of 1996, a federal law that protects patients' health information and gives them rights over their health records. You see, faxes aren't susceptible to getting hacked like emails are—hence, the medical profession's continued use of them.

Crooks are getting more sophisticated. One of their more devious stunts is called "spoofing." That's where they make a number look like yours—you know, as in the same area code and first three digits (the prefix)—so you'll pick up, thinking it's a local call and important. I'm fully aware of this ploy, yet I'll still answer to see whether it's someone important (not that a number that looks like mine is necessarily more important than any other).

Often, these scams originate offshore. That means there's not a lot the law lets us do about them. Although you can install call-blocker software, that's only so effective. But sometimes you *can* take action. Sometimes, in addition to knowing enough to avoid trouble, you can use the law against robocallers to make them pay *you*.

The Telephone Consumer Protection Act was signed into law in 1991. It was one of two federal rules covering telephone communications in the United States. The other was the FTC's Telemarketing Sales Rule, which sets limits on the times telemarketers may call consumers, prohibits calls to a consumer who has asked not to be called again, and sets payment restrictions for the sale of certain goods and services.

Among other proscriptions, the TCPA bans telemarketers, banks, debt collectors, and other companies from using an automatic telephone dialing system (ATDS) to call consumers on a cell phone without their express written consent. The TCPA's purpose was to prevent automated or prerecorded calls except when the recipient consents to receiving them or when the calls are made for an emergency.

Because violation of the TCPA hinges on the involvement of an ATDS, let's discuss what an ATDS is. An ATDS is an autodialer—a dialing system that has the capacity to dial or text numbers without human intervention.

But notice I said "capacity" to dial or text. According to several courts around the country, it doesn't matter whether a company uses the autodialing mode on an autodialer. If the autodialer has the *capacity* to dial without human intervention, all calls placed from that system are subject to the TCPA's express written consent requirement.

If the TCPA requires your express written consent for ATDS-made (or robodialed) calls, how do companies get it? First, let's discuss what express written consent isn't. Simply giving your number to a company does *not* equate to your giving express written consent for them to robocall you. Companies still must request and receive your permission before using an autodialer for sales purposes.

This express written consent disclosure must be clear and conspicuous (Congress phrased the following quote in the affirmative, but you'll get the drift):

> Any person or entity making telephone solicitations (or on whose behalf telephone solicitations are made) will not be liable for violating this requirement if:
>
> ***
>
> It has obtained the subscriber's prior express invitation or permission. Such permission must be evidenced by a signed, written agreement between the consumer and seller which states that the consumer agrees to be contacted by

> this seller and includes the telephone number to which the calls may be placed....
>
> 47 C.F.R. § 64.1200(c)(2)(ii).

I don't know about you, but I can't recall ever giving this sort of express written consent for anyone to call me. But wait, there's more. The TCPA lists several requirements in addition to the robodialer rules. For instance, callers must accept and honor customers' do-not-call requests, can only place calls or send texts between 8:00 a.m. and 9:00 p.m. local time for the recipient, and must treat texts the same as calls when using an ATDS.

Though the Federal Communication Commission and state attorneys general can enforce the TCPA, the greatest risk to companies for violating the TCPA is a class-action lawsuit. (We'll dig into the importance of class actions in Chapter 21.) Often, TCPA class actions result in multimillion-dollar settlements because the scale and scope of a company's violation of the TCPA allows for actual damages, which are rare, or fines of $500 per call, whichever is greater. If a company knowingly violated the TCPA, that amount can triple to $1,500 per willful violation.

Here are a few of the leading TCPA class-action settlements of late:

In re Capital One Telephone Consumer Protection Act Litigation, MDL 2416 (N.D. Ill.)	$75.46 million
Jenkins v. National Grid USA Serv. Co., Inc., No. 15-cv-1219 (E.D.N.Y.)	$38.5 million
Buchanan v. Sirius XM Radio, Inc, No. 3:17-CV-0728-D (N.D. Tex.)	$32.4 million

Brown v. DirecTV, LLC, No. 2:13-cv-01170 (C.D. Cal.)	$17 million
Thomas v. Dun & Bradstreet Credibility Corp., No. 2:14-CV-03194 (C.D. Cal.)	$10.5 million

Individual settlements occur too. Those happen when the cases might not be susceptible to a class action, but the defendant still wants to settle. I've seen individual TCPA settlements range anywhere from $100,000 to as high as $300,000.

As you can see, the TCPA is a powerful tool for putting pesky robocallers in their place. Mind you, not every robocaller has assets or is even onshore. But to the extent they are, you might now have the ability to hit the robocallers where it hurts.

Chapter 14

How to keep an unreasonable landlord honest

We've all had unreasonable landlords, right? Okay, let's call them what they are: landlords we can't stand. They won't fix the toilet, the carpet is stained when it was supposed to be cleaned, and the air blows cold in the winter and hot in the summer. The list goes on. It doesn't really matter *how* your landlord is unreasonable; what matters is *that* your landlord is unreasonable.

Your relationship with your landlord (or leasing office, which is pretty much the same thing) is a contractual one. It's called a landlord-tenant relationship, and it's governed by your lease—the document you probably either skimmed or didn't read at all because, well, it's long. Or maybe you didn't read it because your landlord "conveniently" sent it as a Docusign, which favors the sender (in this case, your landlord) because it's formatted in such a way as to discourage you from reading it: "Just scroll and sign. We'll even provide a happy-looking signature font, followed by an invitation to download the lease but only *after* you've signed it."

All this means you end up with a lease you've never read, that would take time to understand if you had, and, either way, favors your landlord. So what's a tenant to do when something goes wrong or when your landlord leans on you? It turns out that sometimes you can use your landlord's lease against them.

The best way for me to showcase standing up against a landlord and using their lease against them is through another real-life example, where I've again massaged the facts to protect the guilty. Notably, none of what I'm about to tell you is protected by the attorney-client privilege, as my story unfolds in a letter I sent to the landlord's lawyer. Because my letter was to him and not to my clients, its contents aren't privileged.

My story begins with three college roommates—family friends of ours. Perfectly nice guys who rented a house on campus for the school year. Or, put another way, guys whom the scumbag landlord saw coming from a million miles away.

As you'd expect, my clients had a party or two (or three) but nothing significant. The neighbors never complained, and the campus police never showed up. Nevertheless, only a few weeks into the first semester, the landlord started giving my clients trouble about issues that didn't exist.

Eventually, the landlord sent my clients a letter accusing them of breaking the lease that they never read. But if that weren't enough, the landlord included an invoice for $30,000! He claimed they had done that much in damage in the few short weeks they lived there.

When the guys called me for help, which I gave them for free, of course, the first thing I did was review the lease. I took an extraordinarily granular look at it—the kind of look that would make your eyeballs roll back in your head.

Was the lease dense? Yes. Was it cripplingly long? Yes. But was it replete with inconsistencies, carelessness, and opportunities for me to use it against the landlord? Yes! It was only by putting in the work that I unearthed the nuggets I did, which, when assembled, painted a powerful picture favoring my clients.

In keeping with my penchant for showing and not merely telling, what follows is my actual letter to the landlord's lawyer (complete with footnotes though not exhibits), as I believe, again, that often the best way to appreciate the power of the law is to see it in action. My hope is that my letter will provide you with insights, concepts, and soundbites if *you* ever have to write a similar one.

As you read my letter, notice how I channeled all the facts through the terms of the lease the *landlord* wrote. And no sandwich technique here because the landlord was clearly up to no good.

> Dear Attorney Newman,
>
> This letter is in response to the January 27, 2024, email from Elaine Bennes, real-estate agent acting on behalf of George Costanza, Trustee of Constanza Trust dated May 14, 1998 ("Landlord"), threatening legal action against Jerry Seinfeld, Cosmo Kramer, and Larry David ("Tenants"; Landlord and Tenants are hereafter referred to as the "Parties") relating to their rental of 129 W 81st St, New York, NY (the "Property").

On or about June 24, 2023, Tenants contracted with Landlord to rent the Property according to the terms contained in the Parties' Residential Lease ("Lease"). Ex. A. Material to Bennes's January 27, 2024, email, are the following Lease terms

- Paragraph 9—PETS/SERVICE ANIMALS ("$500 per month per animal *for each month violation exists*...."(emphasis added));
- Paragraph 10—MAINTENANCE: A. By Tenant ("Tenant is responsible for *keeping* plumbing fixtures clean [and] sanitary...." (emphasis added));
- Paragraph 10—B. By Landlord ("Landlord/ Agent is responsible for replacement of or repairs to *structural elements* of the building... *major appliances*...and...*heating systems*. Structural elements include, but are *not* limited to,...floor, and ceiling systems, bearing walls and partitions; all interior staircarriage systems;...all hand railings...." (emphasis added));
- Paragraph 22—COURT AWARDED LEGAL FEES ("*In an action* by the Landlord to recover possession of the leased premises...the Tenant is obligated to pay...attorney fees *awarded by a court*. (emphasis added)); and
- Paragraph 26—MOVE-OUT INSPECTION/ SURRENDER OF PREMISES ("Tenant

will *not* paint marks, plaster holds, crevices or cracks; or attempt any repair of the premises without Landlord/Agent's prior written consent." (emphasis added)).

On or about August 24, 2023, Landlord conducted an *ex parte* Property Inspection Report ("Report"). Ex. B. The Report provides two fields for various elements of the Property: OK and NOT OK, yet the Report fails to describe or explain by what standard "OK" was judged, gauged, or quantified—e.g., new construction, older home, collegiate housing.

Following a series of disputes, the Parties, on or about November 5, 2023, agreed to terminate Tenants' tenancy, effective January 31, 2024, via an Irrevocable Vacate and Lease Termination Agreement ("Termination Agreement"). Ex. C. The Termination Agreement, drafted by Landlord, "resolves all disputes with Landlord, even though the Parties may not agree on the underlying facts." *Id.* at 1. The Termination Agreement also makes the recovery of any attorneys' fees contingent upon receiving "a *money judgment* for…attorneys' fees…." *Id.* at 2 (emphasis added).

Furthermore, according to paragraph 3.a., "Landlord agrees to waive all property damage through the Effective Date[, meaning November 5, 2023]." In particular, Landlord agreed, via paragraph 3.a., to waive the alleged

$4,250 in property damages "beyond ordinary wear and tear." *Id.* at 2.[8]

On or about December 3, 2023, and before Tenants vacated the premises, they paid Del Boca Vista Heating & Air Conditioning $185 to repair a faulty thermostat and check the heating, which processes were part of the Premises' HVAC system. Ex. D. *See also* Ex. E (photo taken by Tenants on or about December 3, 2023, depicting dangerously low room temperature reflected on Landlord's broken thermostat).

When Tenants requested from Ms. Bennes reimbursement of this $185, she declined, claiming it was subject to the Lease's $250 deductible even though paragraph 10.B. of the Lease makes Landlord "responsible for replacement of or repairs to…heating systems."

On or about February 9, 2023, Landlord enlisted contractor J. Peterman to prepare an invoice for certain alleged repairs to the Property.[9] Ex. F. Though Mr. Peterman's invoice describes various repair items, it does not indicate the dollar values assignable to each of these items and instead merely presents a lump sum of $17,470.

---

8 Landlord did not provide Tenants a ledger or any evidence of Landlord's alleged $4,250 in damage beyond wear and tear.

9 It is unclear whether Mr. Peterman completed the work described in his invoice or his invoice is merely an estimate.

Finally, in a series of emails from Ms. Bennes to Tenants, commencing January 27, 2024, Ex. G, she ascribes the matters set forth in Mr. Peterman's invoice to Tenants along with charges for additional items. Her January 27, 2024, email included two Dropbox links, to attach photographs of purported damage caused by Tenants, though she did not include "before" photos, and the photos fail to depict damage in breach of the Parties' Lease in that many of the alleged damages involved items for which the Lease makes Landlord responsible or for which Landlord waived any damages claim. In this manner, Ms. Bennes failed to provide sufficient foundation to demonstrate the time the photos were taken, by whom they were taken, and precisely what they depicted, including, as mentioned, a plausible suggestion that they demonstrated Tenants' breach of contract.

[That was the wind-up. Now, here's the pitch.]

Taken together, several problems exist with respect to the damages to which Landlord claims entitlement via Ms. Bennes's series of emails and Mr. Peterman's nonitemized invoice:

1. No photos exist to demonstrate the Property's move-in condition as compared to its move-out condition. Indeed, certain elements of the Property could

have been in *better* condition upon move-out. As it concerns the refuse in various rooms, that's nothing a move-out cleaning service can't resolve.

2. On account of No. 1, Landlord's several photos taken following the Termination Agreement necessarily cannot demonstrate any change in the Property's condition. Additionally, these photos fail to credibly demonstrate material changes in the Property's condition during the mere two months between execution of the Termination Agreement, which included broad Landlord-drafted waiver language, and move-out—days during which no social gatherings occurred and Tenants were aware of and paid special mind to their need to preserve the Property's condition in advance of move-out. What's more, Tenants were out of town for winter break for half of this time.
3. The Lease required Landlord—*not Tenants*—to repair "structural elements," meaning damage to "floor and ceiling systems [and] bearing walls and partitions," Ex. A at ¶ 10.B, meaning the several allegedly new blemishes to the floor, walls, and ceiling described in Ms. Bennes's January 27, 2024, email, and Mr. Peterman's nonitemized invoice he prepared after the Parties' negotiated

Termination Agreement that included Landlord-drafted waiver language, are not plausibly attributable to Tenants. What's more, the Lease prevented Tenants from repairing these items for which Landlord cannot demonstrate Tenants' responsibility. *Id.* at ¶ 26.A. ("Tenant will not paint marks, plaster holds, crevices or cracks; or attempt any repair of the premises without Landlord/Agent's prior written consent.").

4. The thermostat was part of the Property's heating system and thus was not subject to the deductible described in the Lease at ¶ 41.B. Subjecting Tenants to dangerously low temperatures in the dead of winter constitutes a breach of the Landlord's implied warranty of habitability. *See Kramerica Indus. v. Monk's Cafe*, 145 F.3d 619, 621 (2d Cir. 2011) (holding implied warranty of habitability must be read into every residential lease). Accordingly, Landlord must reimburse Tenants the $185 reflected in the invoice from Del Boca Vista Heating & Air Conditioning, Ex. G, in exchange for which Tenants will waive their implied warranty of habitability claim.
5. The Inspection Report contains no indication of smoke detectors despite several opportunities for it when describing each

bedroom. Instead, *no* smoke detectors were present, and Tenants installed their own, which they rightly removed upon vacating the premises.

6. Despite Landlord's assumption that a cat was on the premises for the duration of the Lease, no evidence exists to demonstrate whether (a) a cat was on the premises, (b) the duration of any supposed cat's stay, including whether such supposed stay was merely for a day, an hour, or a minute, or (c) whether Tenants even owned a cat.
7. The microwave is an appliance, meaning it was Landlord's (and Ms. Bennes's) responsibility to repair it. *See* Lease at ¶ 10.B. ("Landlord/Agent is responsible for replacement of or repairs to structural elements of the building...major appliances....").
8. Had smoking occurred, which neither a lone cigarette butt nor the alleged smell of smoke suitably demonstrates, such activities do not give rise to quantifiable damages.
9. Though Ms. Bennes's January 27, 2024, email accuses Tenants of stealing bi-fold doors that fell off (and didn't break) and Tenants left on the back patio; a bed frame that Tenants left in a bedroom; kitchen utensils that Landlord doesn't

describe; and breaking a piece of clay pottery and two door panels, no evidence exist to demonstrate the existence or condition of these items upon move-in. Plus, that Tenants would raid and break various random items during the mere weeks following the execution of the Parties' Termination Agreement (from which time they were studying for finals and refraining from conducting measurable social activities) is implausible.

10. The $17,470 nonitemized estimate contained in Mr. Peterman's invoice eclipses Landlord's $4,250 estimate described in the Termination Agreement. Yet only a couple of months interceded—months during which Tenants were studying for finals and refraining from conducting measurable social activities. Plus, the Lease at ¶ 10.B. makes Landlord—not Tenants—responsible "for replacement of or repairs" to the floors, ceiling, and handrails issues that comprise most of Mr. Peterman's nonitemized invoice.
11. Mr. Peterman's nonitemized invoice purports to describe damage, yet no evidence exists that such conditions did not predate Tenants' occupancy. This would mean Tenants did not breach their obligation to keep plumbing fixtures—arguably, the shower and other

tubs described in the Invoice (Ex. F at 1) clean and sanitary, which obligations caulking does not invoke.

12. Not only are attorneys' fees not recoverable generally, *see, e.g., Mackinaw Peaches v. Sunshine Carpet Cleaners*, 272 F.2d 612, 615 (2d. Cir. 1991) ("[I]n this country attorney's fees usually are not recoverable as an element of damages...."), the Lease makes them recoverable only following successful litigation. *See* Lease at ¶ 21("In an action by the Landlord to recover possession of the leased premises...the Tenant is obligated to pay...attorney fees awarded by a court."). Indeed, in litigation, "[i]f the *Tenant* is the prevailing party, the landlord is obligated to pay the *tenant's* attorney's fees as awarded by the court." *Id.* (emphasis added).

Considering the foregoing, Tenants make the following offer of compromise:

1. Because Tenants encouraged Landlord to use their $7,000 security deposit to satisfy their January rent obligation, they propose netting out this amount, lest they pay $7,000 to Landlord only for Landlord to pay them $7,000 afterward.
2. Understanding that No. 1 satisfies Tenant's January rent obligation, they

do not owe Landlord the $350 late-payment penalty.

3. Because no evidence of cat occupancy exists, Tenants do not owe Landlord $2,000 for four months of unpaid pet rent.
4. Because legal expenses (really, fees) are not recoverable in the U.S. judicial system, Tenants do not owe Landlord $1,607.50 in nonitemized legal fees. Concomitantly, Tenants will not pursue legal fees from Landlord.
5. Because Tenants were not contractually obligated to pay their $419 gas bill, they do not owe Landlord this amount.
6. Because Tenants were contractually obligated to pay their water bill, they will pay Landlord $638.28 for the unpaid water bill.
7. Because Mr. Peterman's $17,470 nonitemized invoices purports to cover items that were Landlord's obligation to repair, items for which insufficient evidence of Tenants' fault exists, and items covered by the waiver language contained in the Parties' Termination Agreement, Tenants do not owe Landlord for any of this invoice absent more specific and convincing proof of fault.

Taken together, for full and complete resolution of the Parties' dispute, which resolution

> the Parties will document in a settlement and release, Tenants offer to pay Landlord $638.28.
>
> Kindly contact me with your client's position concerning the foregoing. If we don't receive your client's acceptance by close of business on February 23, 2024, I will file a declaratory judgment action or, should your client file first, respond with a declaratory-judgment counterclaim.
>
> Best personal regards.
>
> Very truly yours,
> *s/Daniel R. Karon*
> Daniel R. Karon

Phew! Maybe not so lovable but respectful *and* a deep dive. And the reduction at the end sure felt good.

Before postgaming my letter, what's the one thing the guys didn't do that would have largely short-circuited their landlord's position? They should have taken a comprehensive video of their house immediately upon move-in! That way, if the landlord said something was broken, they could have responded, "Not so fast. It was this way when we got here, and you never fixed it." In fact, my son just signed a lease, and I told him to do just that.

Now, I wouldn't expect you to derive the same facts and arguments from your lease, and you might not require the same shock-and-awe approach. I'm merely demonstrating that, by reading your legal documents (because you can bet your landlord and their lawyer have) you, too, can come up with not so much legal as *commonsense* arguments that favor you.

Heck, look at my cat argument. It doesn't derive from the law. It derives from scratching my head (pun intended) and asking, "What is the landlord trying to get away with here? It doesn't seem right, so how can I push back against it? What commonsense arguments can I make?"

Indeed, my letter contains very little law. (You'll notice I included only two case citations, and those were for flavor more than anything.) But it's long on observations, inferences, and turning the tables—all things you can do, too, so long as you realize you have the right to question, push hard, and argue your position.

When you do, your landlord is much less likely to push back. Why? Because you're a pain in their neck, and you're not worth it. But we don't care about the reason; we only care about the result. Let your landlord push on someone who'll lie down, because that's not you.

And if you're wondering what came of my letter, here's what happened. You'll remember the landlord demanded $30,000, and I offered him $638.28. He never got back to me. I credited myself with making such good arguments that he had no sensible rejoinder, and it was easier to say nothing than to reengage.

But there's more to the story. Much more. A couple months after I sent my letter, I ran the property address through Zillow, just to remember how it looked. I couldn't believe what I saw. The landlord had renovated the entire place and listed it for sale! It appeared that all the problems he claimed my clients caused were wiped away in the renovation, leading me to conclude that the landlord had kicked out my clients because he was intent on selling the house and wanted them to fund the renovation project.

Put simply, the renovation replaced the materials that were in place when my clients lived there; it didn't repair them. This meant anything my clients would have paid the landlord wouldn't have gone toward fixing anything, as anything fixed would have been torn out in the renovation.

This smacked of incredibly dirty pool. In light of what I'd discovered, having heard nothing from the lawyer strongly suggested his goal was solely to squeeze my clients. And if he ever gets back to me before the statute of limitations expires on his alleged claims—which he won't—I'm going to come down on him like a ton of bricks for this stunt, including alleging fraud.

I have this added argument in my back pocket not because I have a law degree but because I was curious and took a deeper look into the facts. This is something anyone could have done, and it's an approach around which you, too, could shape a commonsense, fairness-based argument that could help stop an overly aggressive landlord in their tracks.

Yes, I know reading your contracts is mind-numbing. But as uninviting as this might be, read them anyway—ideally, before you sign them, not afterward. Because if you read them, when it starts raining, you're likely to be the one with the umbrella, while your friends who don't read them are likely to get wet.

Chapter 15
Identity theft and how to respond to it

You don't need me to tell you that data breaches and resulting identity theft are rampant. Never mind robocalls; a day doesn't go by where I don't receive a made-up email from Microsoft inviting access into my computer, a suspicious link professing to be an unpaid invoice, or an email claiming to be an important Docusign. Boy, do they try to tempt you, and are they ever well-designed! But if you're not expecting an invoice or it's not your IT person requesting access to your laptop, don't go there.

Data breaches are in the headlines all the time. They hit the financial services industry especially hard, considering how much money fraudsters can steal from the data they breach and mine.

Different ways hackers steal your personal data

So how do thieves actually steal your data? Sources of identity theft can range from a complex hacking scheme to simply digging through your garbage (known as "dumpster diving"). Low-tech approaches are the most common and often involve stealing your mail, purse, wallet, or laptop from which thieves can glean your name, address, date of birth, and often Social Security number. The more sophisticated criminals trade massive quantities of credit card numbers and Social Security numbers online.

Company employees can also cause data breaches. Or sometimes criminals open bogus accounts with financial institutions then use those accounts to steal people's identities. Other approaches involve phishing, malware attacks, and pretexting schemes.

Skimming (a technique that creeps me out) involves stealing card information using a card-reading device. Sometimes, the thieves mount a hidden skimming device over an ATM and record debit card numbers. To nab PINs, they mount a tiny camera near the keypad. Even more sinister, some bandits use a PIN overlay pad—a device that resembles the keypad but records PINs.

The common denominator that ties all these schemes together is the culprit's effort to trick someone—possibly you—into providing personally identifiable information or PII.

What hackers do with your stolen data

What fraudsters do with your data depends on their scheme. In a skimming scheme, the hacker might simply load your stolen

PII onto a blank credit or debit card and withdraw cash from an ATM. In other schemes, the fraudsters will take great pains to give the impression that they're you, sometimes even generating fake government-issued IDs. And if a schemer creates a false address for you, they can get your mail and packages without your even knowing.

If a thief gains access to your credit report, they can tell where you keep various accounts. They can then send a change-of-address letter to your banks and credit card companies and have new checks or credit cards sent to them. Maybe they'd even apply for a new credit card in your name.

After this could come credit card purchases and ATM withdrawals. The purchases and withdrawals might be small so as to avoid detection. Or they could be large so the fraudster can maximize his upside before you shut down the cards or account.

What's the best way to avoid a data hack?

A few simple ways exist to minimize (but unfortunately, never avoid) the likelihood of a successful data breach:

- **Protect your PII.** Unless you trust the requestor, don't share your PII over email, the phone, through the mail, or over the Internet. Certainly don't carry your Social Security card in your wallet.
- **Monitor your accounts.** Scour your checking account statement and credit card statements for unauthorized or suspicious transactions. Often (especially in your credit card statements), you'll see unfamiliar charges. Google the description to see whether it jogs your memory. If your kids share your card, ask whether they

recognize the charge. And don't be afraid to call the credit card company to dispute a charge or even shut down a card and request a new one. I know this latter suggestion comes with hassles, such as reinputting lots of saved account numbers, but that's less inconvenient than a fraudster running up thousands of dollars in avoidable charges.

- **Monitor your credit reports.** The three major credit reporting agencies are TransUnion, www.transunion.com; Experian, www.experian.com; and Equifax, www.equifax.com. Routinely monitor these sites and your credit score. If your score takes an inexplicable drop, you might have been hacked. And, importantly, you can set up a credit freeze on all three of these agencies. Unless you're working with a lender, applying for employment, or a landlord is running a credit check, there's no reason for your credit reports to be open and available to hackers. You can always shut off the freeze when needed, then easily turn it back on.
- **Use strong passwords.** This one speaks for itself. Use different passwords for your different accounts. Make them at least eight characters long and include a mix of letters (upper- and lowercase), numbers, and symbols.
- **Protect your devices.** Always use a firewall and virus and spyware protection software. If you don't work with an IT professional, download free software but only from sites you trust.
- **Be careful when using public Wi-Fi.** Because public Wi-Fi is inherently insecure, hackers can easily intercept your online activity and steal sensitive information like passwords and other PII because anyone can connect

without authentication. This makes public Wi-Fi vulnerable to "man-in-the-middle" attacks (a cyberattack where a hacker positions themself between two parties to intercept or alter their data), rogue hotspots (fake networks), and malware distribution. Basically, anyone on the same network can potentially see your online traffic if you've not taken proper security measures.

- **Be aware of scams.** Be wary of scam phone calls (often robocalls) and never give out PII over the phone.
- **Shred documents.** Don't merely throw away sensitive documents. (Remember dumpster divers?) Shred or destroy them instead, especially those containing your personal information, including credit card offers and convenience checks you never used.
- **Report suspicious activity.** Don't wait to report suspicious activity. If something looks fishy, you can place a fraud alert on your credit reports. Also, let your banks and credit card companies know.

Businesses should employ many of these same techniques to protect customers' PII. Business must also advise their employees to use common sense, such as locking filing cabinets, disposing of personal data appropriately, and keeping IT security current. Strong passwords are similarly essential in business, as are computer firewalls and not leaving laptops open or in cars for thieves to steal.

To guard against an inside job, companies can limit and track who has access to computers and customers' PII. Companies can also divide up PII, ensuring that all customers' data is not on a single computer or server.

Finally, despite their best efforts, financial institutions remain on the front lines and need to prepare for the worst because schemers are out there, and they're getting smarter all the time. Companies hit with a data breach class action (and I've been counsel in several) often face massive liability, the theory being that a hacker got through because the institution's security protocols were deficient. For this reason, your financial institutions need to exercise the highest level of vigilance when it comes to protecting your PII. If you're not sure whether they do, just ask them.

***

The hackers will always be out there, lurking and looking for more devious ways to screw us. That's precisely why we need to do the best we can to make this job so difficult for them that they move on to someone else.

Chapter 16

Detecting wage theft and receiving an honest day's pay for an honest day's work

It's not too much to expect an honest day's pay for an honest day's work, but often employers don't read from the same employee handbook. In ways you can't see—and in ways you sometimes can—they pick your pocket by not paying you for what you've earned and what they owe you. This is known as wage theft. Despite the name, this is a civil—not criminal—matter, which is why I'm discussing it in this book.

Employers are required to pay employees for all hours they work. Failing to pay promised wages is a breach of contract. Failing to pay minimum wages or overtime is a violation of the federal law called the Fair Labor Standards Act, 28 U.S.C. § 201. The states have corresponding laws.

When wage theft deprives an employee of overtime pay or minimum wages for each hour worked, they're entitled to bring a claim against their employer for these unpaid wages. Under federal law, the employee could recover double the amount of their unpaid wages, plus attorneys' fees.

So what are some common (and not so common) examples of wage theft?

- Your employer is required to pay you final wages after you've been fired or laid off. Sometimes, employees never see that final paycheck. More often, this tends to happen if the employee is entitled to only a day or two of wages. But, still, they're *your* wages—not your former employer's.
- Your employer isn't allowed to issue you a paycheck that bounces. The failure to pay any wages earned during a pay period is a breach of contract and violates minimum wage laws.
- Hourly employees who are not exempt from the FLSA must be paid a minimum wage. When they work more than forty hours a week, they must be paid overtime. To enforce these laws, employers must keep accurate time records. Dishonest timekeeping can result in employers stealing employees' wages.
- Wage theft occurs when employers make employees keep working after they've clocked out. Donning and doffing (meaning dressing in uniforms or protective clothing to start a shift, then undressing afterward) is considered work time that should occur on the clock.
- A variation of employers failing to pay for hours worked off the clock occurs when they deduct employees' time for meal breaks that they don't take or that are cut short. Many employers automatically deduct thirty minutes of pay for meal breaks even when they know employees are working during part or all of their breaks. For

instance, when a receptionist must stay at their desk while eating lunch, they deserve to be paid.

- An employer falsifying payroll to make it look like employees worked fewer hours than they actually did is wage theft. Often, this occurs when the employer changes the time an employee clocked in and clocked out—a practice known as altering punches.
- Deducting shortages from your wages that aren't your fault is wage theft. Even if a deduction is lawful, it can become unlawful if it causes you to make less than minimum wage.
- Employers can't dip into your tips. As a general rule, tips belong to you, not to your boss. And though your employer might require you to contribute to a tip pool, strict laws govern tip pools, including that your employer can't take a share. So a manager who shares tips is stealing. Indeed, tip theft is one of the most common forms of wage theft.
- Some salaried employees are exempt from minimum wage or overtime law. (Notice, my third bullet described "employees who are *not* exempt.") This means they're not entitled to overtime if they work more than forty hours per week. But this overtime exemption only applies if the employee is legitimately classified as exempt. For instance, calling a store clerk an executive assistant doesn't mean they meet the executive-employee exemption test. Often, employers claim employees are exempt when they don't satisfy this test. Employers deliberately misclassify employees to avoid paying them overtime.

Several years ago, I was involved in a case against a national restaurant chain. They had a practice of making employees clock out around 9:00 p.m. but made them stay till close at 11:00 p.m., tidying up the kitchen and getting ready for the next day.

To placate (or hoodwink) employees (most of whom were high school students), the managers ordered pizza and had pizza parties while they played music and tried to have fun with the cleaning and set-up processes. But pizza and fun or not, this was wage theft, pure and simple.

The case was a long, tough slog, but finally, we prevailed, getting close to $15 million back for the kids whose pockets the company had picked. And, of course, our final order required the company to put an end to its pizza parties.

If that weren't enough, here's another one. Several years ago, I was involved in a donning-and-doffing class action. It involved plant workers who needed to put on safety gear before they took the floor and remove this gear before they went home. To analyze whether a violation occurred under donning-and-doffing law (and, yes, that's actually a thing), I created this checklist through which you, too, can channel your work situation to determine whether you think you might have a donning-and-doffing claim:

- Does your employer have a policy requiring you to change into certain clothing or protective gear at work?
- Does your employer require you to arrive at work a certain amount of time before your shift starts so you can change into work clothes or protective gear?
- Do you spend more than ten minutes per day changing into and out of clothes or protective gear?

If you answered "yes" to these questions, your employer might owe you for this time. You can review your pay stubs to make sure.

And if you're wondering just what types of jobs qualify for donning-and-doffing scrutiny, here's my checklist:

Partial list of jobs

- Police officers
- Firefighters
- Security guards
- Nurses
- Flight attendants
- Chemical company employees
- Food processing employees

Uniforms or apparatuses subject to donning and doffing (generally involving protective equipment and gear)

- Bulletproof vests and utility belts for police officers
- Personal protective equipment (PPE) for firefighters, including fire proximity suits and "turnout gear" (fire-resistant pants, boots, and jackets)
- Hazmat suits for people who work around radiation, chemical agents, and biological agents
- Protective eye gear for people working in construction, carpentry, and manufacturing, such as goggles, safety glasses, and welder's masks
- Coveralls, aprons, gloves, and hairnets for people who work with food

- Protective suits, coveralls, hoods, gloves, boots, and respirators for people who work with dangerous chemicals or in slaughterhouses
- Metal-mesh gloves for people who work with knives, saws, or other blades
- Neoprene aprons, sleeves, and gloves for people who work with chemicals
- Masks, gowns, rubber gloves, and shoe covers for hospital workers or other healthcare workers

There's my rundown of wage theft and what to look for to protect yourself. Maybe you'll recognize some of the signs—hopefully you won't. But you'd never stand for a thief breaking into your home every two weeks and stealing your property, would you? So don't stand for your employer picking your pocket every two weeks by stealing your wages.

Scour your pay stubs to ensure you're getting what you've worked for. Keep track of your punches to make sure they correspond to your pay stubs. And make sure you're not missing out on well-earned overtime pay.

I know calling out your boss is difficult. I've been there. If you detect a problem, talk to your coworkers. Often, there's strength in numbers. And if you decide to file a case (or even a class action), the FLSA instructs that your employer can't retaliate against you:

> The FLSA mandates that it is unlawful for any person to [d]ischarge or in any other manner discriminate against any employee because such employee has filed any complaint or instituted or caused to be instituted any proceeding under or related to this Act, or has testified or

> is about to testify in any such proceeding, or has served or is about to serve on an industry committee.
>
> 29 U.S.C. § 215(a)(3).

Stand tall and do what's necessary to advocate for yourself. If that means raising a ruckus, consider going for it. If you think it's better not to, go find a job where you'll be respected. Either way, now you know your rights. What you do with them is up to you.

Chapter 17

How to recognize and fight off overly aggressive debt collectors

I hope this hasn't happened (and won't happen) to you, but imagine your cell phone rings, and it's an 800 or restricted number. You pick up, and it's a debt collector. Or let's say you go to your mailbox, and an unfamiliar letter is waiting for you. Again, it's from a debt collector.

Because debt collectors had a habit of unfairly leaning on debtors, in 1977, Congress passed the Fair Debt Collection Practices Act (FDCPA). It's a consumer protection statute that provides legal protection from abusive debt collection practices, as stated in the Consumer Credit Protection Act.

The FDCPA's main objectives are to eliminate abusive practices in consumer debt collection and promote fair debt collection. The FDCPA provides consumers with a way to dispute and obtain validation of debt information to ensure its accuracy. It provides guidelines for debt collectors, defines the rights of consumers involved with debt collection, and describes penalties and remedies for debt collectors' violations.

Mind you, the FDCPA doesn't apply to the collection of all debts. It generally applies when third-party collectors seek to collect a debt from a consumer. It doesn't apply to business debts or in-house collection efforts by the entity that extended you credit.

Under the FDCPA, debt collectors can't do a number of things to you:

- **Debt collectors can't harass you.** Harassment means threats of violence, using obscene or profane language, listing your debt for sale to the public, and excessive contact. Debt collectors can't contact you at work after you've asked them not to. Likewise, they can't contact you if you're represented by an attorney or after you've requested a debt-validation letter, which is a document that describes the debt, how much you owe, and to whom, as well as when you need to pay it.

  Aggressive behavior could indicate you're dealing with a scam artist. If a supposed debt collector has a big, ugly mouth, do some digging to be sure you owe this debt in the first place.

- **Debt collectors can't employ unfair practices.** Debt collectors can't deceive you. For example, they can't seek to collect interest, fees, or other charges on top of the amount you owe unless your contract with the creditor (the company you owe money to) allows it. Similarly, if you provide a postdated check, they can't deposit it early, causing it to bounce. And they certainly can't threaten the possibility of jail time or threaten to take your property.

- **Debt collectors can't reveal the existence of your debt to third parties.** Though collection agencies may contact your neighbors, coworkers, or relatives to obtain information such as your address or phone number, they can't otherwise communicate with third parties about your debt, except for your spouse or lawyer. This means if a bill collector contacts your neighbors, coworkers, or relatives, they can't reveal any information about your debt, including the fact that they're calling from a debt collection agency.

That's what debt collectors *can't* do under the FDCPA. What *must* bill collectors do under the FDCPA?

- **Debt collectors must identify themselves and explain that they're calling to collect a debt.** In every communication to the consumer, debt collectors must state their identity and why they're calling. As it concerns collection letters, this language can take various forms, such as, "This is an attempt to collect a debt by Acme Collection Bureau, a debt collector, and any information obtained will be used for that purpose," or "Acme Collection Bureau is a debt collector. We are trying to collect a debt that you owe to Coyote Family Health Centers. We will use any information you give us to help collect that debt," or "This communication is from a debt collector. This is an attempt to collect a debt, and any information obtained will be used for that purpose." Slightly different language; same message.

- **Debt collectors must provide the name and address of the original creditor.** Upon thirty days of your request for a validation letter, debt collectors must provide you with the name of the company to which the debt is owed.
- **Debt collectors must provide verification of the debt.** When you request a verification letter, the debt collector must mail you the requested verification information or cease collection efforts.
- **Debt collectors must lay off if you dispute the debt.** Once you receive the debt collector's notice, you have thirty days to demand the verification letter so you may dispute the amount. If you dispute the debt, the debt collector must stop collection efforts and verify the debt or provide you with a copy of a judgment evidencing the debt.
- **Debt collectors may file a lawsuit only in a proper court.** If a debt collector decides to sue you, it may only file where you live or where you signed the contract giving rise to the debt.

These are the dos and don'ts of debt collecting. Believe me, not all debt collectors follow them. Case in point is a federal class-action FDCPA lawsuit I had a few years ago in Chicago. My case involved a collection agency's misleading foreclosure letters in violation of the FDCPA. Unlike a modest consumer debt, the collector was leaning on people with regard to their homes. You can only imagine how freaked out they were.

My lawsuit alleged that the letters suggested an attorney had reviewed the mortgage holder's accounts when no attorney review occurred. Indeed, no lawyers participated in the process, yet the letters were on attorney letterhead. As a result, the letters miscalculated people's debts by including attorneys' fees when no attorneys had participated in the letters' preparation.

After about five years of litigation for a class of largely inner-city Chicagoans who'd received the collection agency's letters, we settled (meaning, resolved the case short of going to trial) for $8.45 million. This money went straight to people who had overpaid the collection agency or as "statutory damages" under the FDCPA that provided payments of up to $1,000 for each class member. Finally (and importantly), the collection agency agreed to modify its foreclosure letters to remove and clarify misleading or illegal language.

The FDCPA has teeth; my case is proof of that. So if you ever receive a collection call or letter, keep these requirements in mind. And if you believe a debt collector is operating outside the lines, feel free to contact a lawyer to discuss the possibility of an individual case or even a class-action case, like mine.

Chapter 18
Recognizing and rooting out elder claims

Schemers often target our nation's elderly community because of its lack of comfort with technology, spirit for cooperation, or susceptibility to manipulation. Make no mistake—this is elder abuse.

The US government's Administration for Community Living defines elder abuse as "any knowing, intentional, or negligent act by a caregiver or any other person that causes harm or a serious risk of harm to a vulnerable adult."[10] Also, the Federal Trade Commission (FTC) brings enforcement actions to stop unlawful practices and, when possible, to return money to elderly victims.[11] And until recently, the Consumer Financial Protection Bureau (CFPB) offered valuable resources to combat

---

10 "What Is Elder Abuse," Administration for Community Living, last modified January 31, 2019, https://acl.gov/programs/elder-justice/what-elder-abuse.

11 "Protecting Older Consumers 2023-2024," Federal Trade Commission, October 18, 2024, https://www.ftc.gov/system/files/ftc_gov/pdf/federal-trade-commission-protecting-older-adults-report_102024.pdf.

elder abuse.[12] As of this book's publication, the CFPB's status is in flux, with legal battles and leadership changes impacting its operations. As such, it's uncertain how aggressive the CFPB's abuse enforcement will remain.

Elder abusers can be family members, friends, or caregivers. Every state has some form of elder abuse prevention laws. And though laws and definitions of terms vary among the states, exploitation, which according to the Administration for Community Living, means "the illegal taking, misuse, or concealment of funds, property, or assets of a senior for someone else's benefit," fits the bill.

You needn't appeal to and wait on the state or federal government to help when you or your loved one is an elder-abuse victim. Civil remedies—meaning remedies *you* can initiate—are at your disposal. But first, it's important to identify the common types of elder-abuse schemes in the marketplace.

> **Securities Fraud.** Often, seniors are victims of financial scams involving securities fraud. They should never bite when someone cold calls them or solicits them for investments (i.e., parting with their hard-earned retirement funds), whether by phone, mail, online, or in person. Sure, they'll hear glowing promises of fantastic returns, but that's an even bigger red flag that someone is selling them a pyramid or Ponzi scheme. I share office space with lawyers who pursue Ponzi schemers, and I don't think I've seen an uglier and more sinister apparatus. In these schemes, though the returns look good,

12 "Protecting Older Adults from Fraud and Financial Exploitation," Consumer Financial Protection Bureau, accessed March 3, 2025, https://www.consumerfinance.gov/consumer-tools/educator-tools/resources-for-older-adults/protecting-against-fraud.

come day's end, the only person who profits is the Ponzi schemer.

As for legitimate securities, pump-and-dump schemes involve brokers who aggressively promote a stock, out of proportion to its potential for growth. After the broker collects their fees and the stock price soars, they sell it. Then, when the stock collapses (as it almost always does), the broker is nowhere to be found, and neither is the victim's money.

Telemarketing schemes. Often, telemarketing schemes occur in the context of robocalls. Seniors tend to be especially vulnerable to these schemes. Not only should they never participate in a cold-call conversation, but also they should never give their credit card number or other PII. And they should never purchase gift cards, then provide the scratch-off code. Finally, they should never do anything to allow access to their computer, where important passwords and financial information might reside. Nothing good ever comes from doing these things.

Mortgage fraud scams. Mortgage fraud scams often involve reverse mortgages. You've seen the commercials on TV. A reverse mortgage is a type of financing for your home that allows seniors to supplement their income through their home's equity. (I sound like the commercials, right?) Unlike traditional mortgages, borrowers aren't required to make monthly payments. Instead, the lender makes these payments to the borrower and takes a lien on the borrower's home. The loan is repaid when the borrower sells their home, refinances it, permanently moves out, or dies.

Reverse mortgages are only available to homeowners who are at least sixty-two years old, and lenders must follow all of the same regulations that apply to other mortgages, including the three-day right to cancel the loan. But it's precisely because reverse mortgages are only available to seniors that these loans are susceptible to manipulation, overselling, and other forms of fraud.

Fake contests and sweepstakes. Receiving a notice in the mail announcing a prize or free gift should set off bells and whistles. There's no free lunch in this world—period. Yet fake contests and sweepstakes often instruct recipients that they must pay money or give a credit card number to receive their prize.

The sophistication of these schemes has grown exponentially since the advent of the Internet. We've all heard of the "Nigerian prince scam," right? That's the one where you receive an email from a person purporting to live abroad. They claim to be the relative of a Nigerian prince, and they require your assistance moving money out of the country in exchange for a percentage after the job is complete. To achieve this, they request your bank account number to facilitate the money transfer. These scams end only one way—with the victim out a lot of money.

Healthcare fraud. Similar to the Nigerian prince scam are the healthcare fraud scams. These are the robocalls that ask whether you're enrolled in Medicare Part D.

> No matter your answer or what button you press, you're approved, and you're transferred to a supervisor. This scheme usually involves providing authorization to debit your bank account or charge your credit card. Either option is in exchange for nothing.

***

So what do you do if you or a loved one is an elder-fraud victim? You can report the practice to your state attorney general's consumer protection division or the FTC. You can even report it to the Better Business Bureau. You should also contact your banks and credit card issuers and inquire about shutting down the schemers' access and clawing back any funds they've stolen. And you can enlist the help of a consumer attorney to sue civil claims (assuming you can locate the schemers and they have money), whether in an individual case or a class-action lawsuit.

If you're older, now you know what to be on the lookout for. If you have older relatives or friends, now you know what to encourage them to avoid. Either way, now you're empowered to protect yourself against elder claims.

Chapter 19

How to fight a traffic ticket

So you're in traffic court. Ugh! Many of us have been there. If you've decided to fight your traffic ticket (because you *weren't* speeding or you *didn't* run the red light, right?), you have only one chance to convince the judge to dismiss your case. Remember, you'll have an experienced prosecutor sitting or standing across from you—someone who knows the judge well from years of practice and hundreds of cases together. You'll be in the courtroom, stating your case. This means you'll need to pay attention to three essential rules of trial practice: prepare, prepare, and prepare. So let's dig in.

If your ticket doesn't already include a court date, you'll need to request one. The ticket should provide instructions for how to do this.

Then, review your ticket (or citation) and Google (then study) the actual traffic code section you're accused of violating—e.g., speeding, running a red light, or failing to stop for a school bus. Focus on the consequences and whether they could affect your insurance rates, cost you a monetary fine that will affect your pocketbook, or both.

Before you decide whether to contest the ticket, keep in mind, if the judge refuses to dismiss your case and awards traffic violation points and a fine, you might also get hit with court costs. These reimburse the court for maintaining the courthouse, paying court personnel, and maintaining documents and computer systems. These costs could be a hundred or more additional dollars.

When you decide to proceed, you'll need to formulate your defenses. Remember, in this case, you'll be the defendant (throughout this book, I've described situations where you're the *plaintiff*), meaning you need an explanation or basis for encouraging the judge to dismiss the citation. Here are five reliable possibilities:

1. Credibly dispute the police officer's opinion

Traffic court judges have heard every excuse in the book for why the police officer got it wrong. For this reason, you'll want a solid basis for questioning the police officer's opinion of what occurred.

Traffic citations often involve police officers' opinions that drivers were driving unsafely, whether rolling through a stop sign or improperly changing lanes. These citations often require the police officer's opinion as to what happened, whose judgment you can challenge.

For instance, let's say you were cited for an improper lane change. All the police officer saw was your lane change; they didn't see the compact car sticking out of the shoulder that you wanted to avoid for everyone's safety. Perhaps they didn't see the massive pothole you wanted to avoid. Or maybe something fell off a truck in front of you, and you wanted to avoid that.

To bolster your argument, what if the police officer was driving in *front* of you and couldn't have seen any of these things? Is it plausible for the court to believe the police officer was paying more attention to what he could poorly see in the rearview mirror than to the road ahead?

Turning to speeding tickets, in some states, the posted speed limit is not always the law. In these states, you can travel at a safe speed if road and traffic conditions permit. If you got a speeding ticket under these circumstances, you could challenge the police officer's opinion of the road and traffic conditions to prove your speed was safe. An example might be if you were driving seventy miles per hour in a sixty-mile-per-hour zone because traffic was also traveling at seventy miles per hour. Driving at sixty miles per hour would have been unsafe, which is why you weren't doing it.

2. Dispute the way the police officer presented evidence

This technique requires considerable skill and care to perform credibly. Certain citations are clear-cut and are not subject to questioning a police officer's judgment—take running a stop sign, failing to stop for a school bus, or making an illegal U-turn. On the surface, these infractions seem pretty cut-and-dried.

These are tough cases to challenge, but it's not impossible. In these cases, you don't challenge them by questioning the officer's judgment. You use the back door, meaning you provide *other* evidence that calls into question the police officer's observations. Here are a few things I've used—sometimes with success, sometimes without:

Gather eyewitness statements. If someone else was in your car, get their statement. Granted, the prosecutor will allege bias, but it's better than nothing, and the prosecutor has the burden of proof—often beyond a reasonable doubt, which is pretty high. So punch holes in their story.

Also, if the citation lists any witnesses, call them. Ask them what happened and get their statements beforehand. Perhaps the judge will consider their statements. If the witnesses' statements don't serve you, don't introduce them.

Take photographs. Many of my cases involve business disputes. This means the facts of the story are buried in millions of pages of electronic documents. But in a traffic situation, the facts are often the highway, signs or traffic lights, and vehicles.

The police officer will be describing the situation to the judge. But what if the police officer got it slightly wrong? The only way you can dispute this is by providing pictures, whether still or by video. Pictures can show your claim clearly. They can show dangerous road conditions that caused your U-turn, the massive pothole that caused your abrupt lane change, or the shrubbery that obscured the stop sign.

But be sure to take your photos and videos right away. If you miss out, be sure to take them at the same time the next day, as this could be your best reasonable proxy. The judge is sure to grill you on the facts behind your photos and videos.

Diagrams. Often, traffic citations include little diagrams depicting what happened. Feel free to create your own diagram that shows where your car was in relation to the officer at the time of the ticket. The best diagram would show that the police officer couldn't have seen you run a red light because they were too far behind you to credibly tell. Remember, the prosecutor has the burden of proof. All you have to do is poke holes in their story.

3. Present evidence that the traffic violation was a "mistake of fact"

Sometimes you just understand things wrong. If you can convince the judge that this genuinely happened, you could argue you committed a mistake of fact. "Mistake of fact is a general defense to criminal responsibility." *Mercado v. State*, Nos. 04-22-00555, 2024 Tex. App. LEXIS 4241, at *15 (Tex. App. June 20, 2024). "It is a defense to prosecution that the actor through mistake formed a reasonable belief about a matter of fact if his mistaken belief negated the kind of culpability required for commission of the offense." *Id.* "Unlike many other statutory defenses, mistake of fact negates an element of the offense: the culpable mental state." *Id.*

This defense could come in handy for certain tickets because it emphasizes that you made a mistake about a situation beyond your control. Mistakes of fact mean you honestly and reasonably believed you were following the law, though it doesn't mean you can claim you weren't aware of the law.

An example of a mistake-of-fact defense would be if you were driving the wrong way down a vacant one-way street because the street sign had graffiti on it suggesting you were driving the correct way. Or let's say you drive the same street to work every day, but the night before, the city lowered the speed limit. You missed the change and mistakenly believed the old speed limit still applied. Though this defense might wash, your mistake of fact can't occur beyond a reasonable time after the installation of the new sign. After a reasonable time, you'll be presumed to have seen it, meaning you'll need to obey it.

4. The circumstances justified driving as you did

For this defense, you just fall on your sword and admit to illegal driving. But when doing so, you'll describe why the way you drove was justified. This is a relatively easy defense because it doesn't require you to oppose a police officer or gather elusive evidence.

Let's say someone was tailgating you, but you couldn't switch lanes to get out of the way unless you gunned it and safely slipped into an opening on your right. Or let's say the car to your right began driving erratically, causing you to abruptly cut left to avoid getting hit. In both situations, you were simply trying to keep yourself safe. If there's a record of your calling 911, you'd have an even stronger objective case. Of course, if you continued to swerve or kept speeding, I think you'd agree this defense wouldn't work.

5. Your driving was necessary to prevent harm

This defense resembles the last one, except that your driving was necessary to prevent harm to others. A simple example is swerving to avoid a child running into the street or someone stepping off the sidewalk. In these settings, evasive action would be necessary to avoid critically harming someone. You'll need to prove to the judge that, had you not driven this way, you *would* have harmed someone, but that could be difficult, especially without a witness.

Ineffective defenses (a.k.a. what not to do)

I'm not a traffic attorney, but I've participated in enough traffic hearings as a defendant to know what *not* to say to a judge. Here are a few of the worst-ofs:

- **Don't claim ignorance of the traffic laws.** Don't say you weren't aware of the speed limit or other traffic laws. If you aren't aware of them, you don't deserve to be driving. You're required to know the traffic laws, and this "defense" will never work.
- **Don't look for a loophole.** Sometimes police officers spell your name wrong. Don't use that as a basis to argue they have the wrong person. Minor errors on a traffic ticket usually don't invalidate it.
- **Don't fake a personal emergency.** Don't say you were speeding due to a personal emergency. If you go that route, believe me, the judge will press you for proof you can't produce. It isn't often a viable defense without strong evidence, and you won't have it.
- **Don't tell the judge, "This is how they do it where *I* used to live."** This one's my personal favorite, so to speak. Shortly after we moved to Cleveland from Chicago, I got a ticket for blowing past a school bus stop sign. (I hadn't seen one in so long, I literally spaced

what to do.) I showed up in court to contest the ticket. (How I thought I'd win *that* one, I dunno!) When pleading my case, I told the judge that professional courtesy, as I'd experienced in Chicago traffic court, encouraged her to dismiss the ticket. She leaned forward, leered at me over her glasses, and growled, "Counselor, you're not in Chicago anymore." She banged her gavel. The crack of wood on wood echoed off the courtroom walls. "Welcome to Cleveland, Dorothy. Full fine and court costs. Bailiff, call the next case." What's the lesson in all this? Ignore what you see on the television courtroom shows. It's *not* your courtroom, and you *never* tell the judge what to do.

Let's say you actually were speeding or ran the stop sign. What are your options in traffic court?

If you really did break the law and are concerned about paying the citation and perhaps getting points, you can still show up to traffic court. There, your choices will be to plead not guilty or plead what's called *nolo contendere*. (If you intend to plead guilty, there's no reason to show up in traffic court.)

The main difference between pleading not guilty and pleading *nolo contendere*, which is Latin for "I do not wish to contend," is that a not guilty plea means you deny the charges against you, while a *nolo contendere* plea means you accept the penalty without admitting guilt.

More precisely, if you plead not guilty, it means you request a trial where the prosecution will intend to prove its case beyond a reasonable doubt (in most states). But if you plead *nolo contendere* (or no contest, as it's more casually called), you neither admit nor deny the charges, yet you accept the court's penalty as if you were guilty. A no contest plea, which I've taken before, can be a good option if you're concerned about the reputational impact of pleading guilty or being found guilty.

Also important about a no contest plea is that it avoids giving a person you may have hit with your car the benefit and power of a guilty plea in a possible civil case for money damages. That said, a no contest plea could still be considered a conviction, which could make it challenging finding a job, getting into school, or getting licensed.

***

So there are some nuts and bolts about traffic court. They're the rules of the road I live and drive by.

Chapter 20
What's involved in going to small claims court?

Throughout this book, I've emphasized the importance and effectiveness of writing letters. But sometimes (even often) letters don't work. That's when you need to ratchet things up. That's when you need to take 'em to court—likely, small claims court.

Small claims court is perfect for small-value consumer claims. You can represent yourself (called *pro se*), the rules are relaxed, the court clerks are generally helpful (because they know you're *pro se*), and the filing fee is much lower than if you were to file your claim in the "higher" court, meaning the court that allows claims for a higher jurisdictional amount.

Depending on the small claims court, the jurisdictional maximum can range anywhere from $6,000 (as in Ohio) to $20,000 (as in Minnesota). Perfect for small value—yet important—consumer claims.

Most small claims courts post their filing requirements online. They're not onerous, and if you're considering filing in small claims court, it's essential that you read them. For example, here's a link to what's required for filing a small claim in Cleveland, Ohio: https://clevelandmunicipalcourt.org/clerk-of-courts/civil-division/how-to-file-a-small-claim---new. But because it's one thing to merely cite a practice and another to walk through the practice and its related concepts to help ensure understanding, let's do the latter.

The demand letter requirement in some small claims court

As a prerequisite to filing a small claim, many jurisdictions require a plaintiff to send a demand letter to the defendant. A demand letter is what I've been providing throughout this book—it demands from the defendant what you intend to seek in damages, whether in small claims court or a higher court.

Though some jurisdictions allow plaintiffs to make a verbal demand, it's still smart to send a written demand as it prevents the defendant from denying they received your demand or claiming you demanded less than you end up claiming in court. If anything, you've learned by now that I'm a sucker for putting everything in writing!

As you've seen from *my* letters, your demand letter should describe your dispute with the defendant and explain how and why you deserve relief. Be sure to include documents that prove your claim, including materials that describe facts, specify dates, calculate dollar amounts, and explain the participants in transactions. Also include a drop-dead date by which you intend to file a small claim if the defendant doesn't pay you the sum or money (or take the corrective action) you require.

Importantly, realize the judge will likely see this letter, which is supposed to be your reasonable attempt to compromise and stay out of their court. Indeed, with all letters, the ultimate audience could be a judge. That's why your letters can never be discourteous or disrespectful. Sure, you can be passionate, but be passionate with class. Don't fight with the other side. Judges hate that. They compare it to a parent watching their kids fight. Many of us know the reaction *that* evokes. Let the other side fight. You're there to solve your problem—not to make it worse.

And although the judge isn't expecting you to have an attorney's expertise, the judge *does* expect you to use a professional tone in their court. Related to that, be sure to proofread your letter to ensure it has no typos or grammatical gaffes. If writing isn't your strong suit, have a friend whose strong suit it is read it. The judge likely won't cut you a break if your letter and eventual complaint are full of typos. Remember, you're always writing for the court. And the more well-spoken, organized, and professional you are, the more seriously the court will take you.

Finally, because each state's small claims rules are different, read them (as I mentioned above) to ensure that you're sending to the defendant precisely what the court requires. Failure to comply with the court's rules may result in the clerk of court rejecting your complaint.

So your presuit demand letter didn't work—now what?

If your demand letter falls flat, it's time to file your lawsuit in small claims court. After all, if you threaten to sue, you'd better do it unless you want to kiss goodbye your possibility of recovery.

You have several choices to consider when filing your lawsuit. The first step is to decide on the right court. Each county in your state should maintain its own small claims court department, and you'll need to research which department is appropriate. Some courts are busier than others. This could affect how long the judge will take to hear your case.

Also (and critically), legal claims, no matter how small, are subject to statutes of limitations. Those are deadlines beyond which you can no longer sue. If you're preparing a small claim, you'd best research that claim's statute of limitations to ensure that you file your lawsuit before the statute of limitations lapses.

The next step is to jump onto the appropriate small claims court's website to identify and complete the form (or forms) necessary to file your small claim. Again, if you get confused or otherwise messed up, the small claims clerks of court are often very friendly and helpful.

How do you list—or name—the defendant in your small claims complaint?

Properly naming the person or business (i.e., the defendant) in your small claim matters. If the defendant is a person, you can simply list their name. If the defendant is a business, it couldn't hurt to name the business and the person there who screwed you—kind of a belt-and-suspenders approach that makes sure you've named the right defendant in case it turns out the business isn't responsible.

We do this all the time in price-fixing class actions: We name as defendants the company *and* the people there who were responsible for the price fixing. Granted, these cases involve larger stakes, but they're conceptually the same. Because if you don't name everyone up front, it's often impossible to include new parties after the statute of limitations has passed.

After you file your complaint and pay a modest filing fee, you'll need to notify the defendant that you've sued them. This is known as *serving* the defendant, and it involves precise rules. If you've not properly served someone with a lawsuit, it violates due process for you to collect a judgment from them.

To give you a feel for what the service rules look like, here's an excerpt from Federal Rule of Civil Procedure 4. (The Federal Rules govern attorneys' conduct in federal courts nationwide—*not* state courts, which include small claims courts):

> (e) SERVING AN INDIVIDUAL WITHIN A JUDICIAL DISTRICT OF THE UNITED STATES. Unless federal law provides otherwise, an individual—other than a minor, an incompetent person, or a person whose waiver has been filed—may be served in a judicial district of the United States by:
>
> (1) following state law for serving a summons in an action brought in courts of general jurisdiction in the state where the district court is located or where service is made; or
>
> (2) doing any of the following:
>
> (A) delivering a copy of the summons and of the complaint to the individual personally;
>
> (B) leaving a copy of each at the individual's dwelling or usual place of abode with someone of suitable age and discretion who resides there; or

(C) delivering a copy of each to an agent authorized by appointment or by law to receive service of process.

You will want to research your jurisdiction's service rules because, again, defective service can grind your lawsuit to a halt before it gets off the ground. *See, e.g., Michael Young v. Wis. Dep't of Corr. Div. of Cmty. Corr., No. 23-CV-1200, 2023 U.S. Dist. LEXIS 207267, at *16 (E.D. Wis. Nov. 20, 2023)* ("Defendants are also correct that defective service may be a basis for dismissal; to comport with due process"); *Phillips v. Life Prop. Mgmt. Servs., No. 21-11350, 2021 U.S. App. LEXIS 34627, at *3 (11th Cir. Nov. 22, 2021)* ("[T]he district court did not err in dismissing Phillips's complaint for defective service as to those defendants who were not personally served or did not return a waiver of service.").

How to prepare for your hearing day

After you've filed your case and properly served the defendant, the clerk will assign you a hearing date. At the hearing you can explain your case to the judge and describe the relief you're seeking. You'll want to prepare for this hearing, including organizing documents and inviting witnesses. You'll also want to anticipate any questions you believe you can expect to hear from the judge. Remember our three rules of trial practice.

Of course, the defendant, if they're smart, will be preparing this same way. That's all the *more* reason to be well-prepared yourself. To this end, in addition to anticipating the court's questions, anticipate your opposition's arguments and have thoughtful responses to everything. If you're in the right, this shouldn't be an insurmountable problem.

If you're anxious about all this, "moot court" the hearing with friends or family members. This involves getting someone to play the judge and someone to play the defendant. Brief them on the facts, even providing them with your documents. Then have your judge conduct a question-answer session where they ask you and the defendant all about the case. This way, when you hear questions in court, you won't hear them for the first time. Familiarity is a great way to avoid nervousness.

As for your witnesses, not only should you make sure they're available and can attend court, but also you should prepare them. You don't want them failing to show up or, if they do show up, telling the story wrong.

In addition to preparing witnesses to tell your story, you'll want to prepare them to push back against the defendant's questions of them—called cross-examination.

If a witness refuses to appear in court, you can serve them with a subpoena. This requires completing a form with the small claims clerk and suitably serving it on the witness before the hearing. If you need to subpoena a witness, it's likely they won't be completely supportive. After all, they don't want to be there or to help you. So bear in mind that if you call a "hostile" or "adverse" witness, it could be *you* doing the cross-examining.

It's hearing day—what can you expect?

Often, logistics derail an otherwise well-prepared and good-looking case. At hearings in federal court, I've seen laptops die, PowerPoint presentations fail, and cell phones drop when lawyers dialed in. Nothing like this will ever happen to you if you're—you know it: prepared.

Stepping back to before your hearing day, it's also smart to scout out the courthouse. Make sure you know where to park and through what door to enter. Make sure you know what's required to pass through security. Often, your courtroom and hearing time will be posted online. If they're not, during your dry run, confirm with the clerk where to go and when.

When you arrive (at least half an hour early) at the courthouse, confirm your hearing time and courtroom. Courts get backed up, and times routinely change. Courtrooms change too—sort of the way gates change at the airport. If you can't find your case or courtroom, ask the clerk.

Often, you can enter the courtroom early to wait. If court is already in session, you can observe your judge. (To play it safe, you could even do this a few days beforehand—*I* would.) You can observe their manner and personality. Are they friendly or mean? Are they attentive or laid back? Are they sticklers for evidence, or do they just want to hear from the parties?

By this time, you'll probably see the defendant sitting in the courtroom too. Are they serene or nervous? Are they alone or do they have witnesses? Are they empty-handed or do they have a stack of documents?

If you think it would matter, you could even invite them into the hallway for one last attempt at resolution. Often, settlements occur "on the courthouse steps," when the stakes are highest and both sides—no matter their posturing or how good they claim to feel about their case—feel the heat. If you end up resolving things, it's a good idea to put your agreement into a signed writing—a.k.a. a settlement agreement.

If you resolve the case, you can dismiss it by letting the court know and filing a notice of dismissal. If you don't, it's game on.

When the court calls your case, you'll approach the bench or take a seat at counsel table. Though you might be worked up, the judge runs the show—not you (as we now know)—so listen to all the judge's instructions and answer all the judge's questions. Again, *don't* do what you often see on the television courtroom programs, meaning don't think you're running the show and *don't* interrupt the judge.

Because you're the plaintiff, the judge will ask you to tell your story first. Next, the defendant will tell their story. Often, the judge will push back on both sides to understand as best possible what happened because, remember, there are *three* sides to every story: yours, theirs, and the truth. Only answer questions you're asked; don't answer questions asked of the defendant and certainly don't interrupt the defendant. But most importantly, always tell the truth. If you don't know an answer, just say so. Don't guess and definitely don't lie.

At the close of the evidence, the judge will either rule from the bench or reserve their ruling and issue a written decision later that the court will circulate by letter or email.

The losing party may appeal the decision to the court that has jurisdiction over the small claims court that heard the case. Though it's unusual for parties to appeal small claims decisions, appeals happen.

My real-life small claims experience

Just as I'm familiar with federal court, I'm familiar with small claims court. I have a friend who plays trombone for a world-renowned orchestra. He also collects trombones. A promising trombone student from Indiana contacted him online about purchasing one of his horns. Eager to put a good instrument at a good price into a young musician's hands, my friend happily agreed to sell him one of his favorite keepsakes.

My friend went to a national shipping store and asked whether they could pack the instrument as necessary to avoid damage. After all, the original packing materials were long gone.

The franchise owner promised the horn would arrive in Indiana intact. He even described the packing technique he would use: bubble wrap surrounded by packing peanuts. This, he promised, would do the trick. Happy with the owner's explanation, my friend paid $159 for shipping-and-packing services and bid his gleaming horn farewell.

Three days later, my friend received a text message from the young Hoosier musician. It included disturbing photos of my friend's trombone, its bell flattened like a pancake.

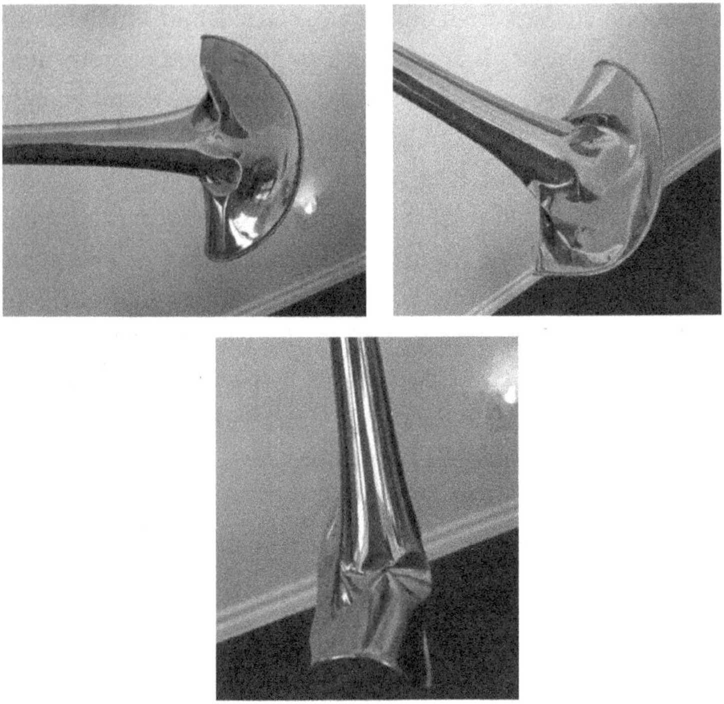

The cause? The shipper *hadn't* packed it as necessary to avoid this damage—specifically, no packing peanuts.

Unwilling to let a young music student take a bath, my friend reimbursed him for the cost of the instrument. Now my friend was out the purchase price—$1,600. Instead of going it alone, he called me. We discussed the facts of his case, and I grabbed the bull by the horn.

I asked my friend for all his documents. They included his text messages and other correspondence to and from his buyer, correspondence with the shipping store, and transactional documents, meaning his contract and receipt from the shipping store.

Reviewing his contract, I didn't notice a forced-arbitration clause (see Chapter 11), so that was a good start. I confirmed this on the company's website. Again, nothing—although, had a forced-arbitration clause existed online, the parties' contract likely would have superseded it.

Next, I reviewed my friend's documents and the company's website for helpful language, and I quickly found it. For loose packages, the company's online Guidelines for Packing called for the use of packing peanuts, explaining that "[d]ue to the manner by which packing peanuts shift and settle, it is essential to use at least three inches of cushioning around the contents of any box containing a loose item."

I dug deeper into the company's website and came across musical instrument requirements. They reemphasized the need for careful packaging, requiring "at least four inches of bubble wrap surrounding the item." Does my friend's photo look like at least three inches of cushioning and four inches of bubble wrap to you?

Considering the website's language about using packing peanuts and bubble wrap, my alternate legal theories were the shipper's breach of contract (it didn't do something my friend paid for, though I didn't need the website's language to know that) and negligence (it had acted carelessly and not in keeping with its own guidelines and requirements establishing its standard of care).

But liability is only half the equation. My next question was damages—namely, what to demand from the shipper *for* its breach of contract and negligence. My friend had paid $159 for packing and shipping services but hadn't gotten what he paid for. I suppose I could have demanded $159.

But that wouldn't even come close to making my friend whole. Instead, I was going to demand the $1,600 on the basis that these damages were a consequence of the shipper's breach ("consequential damages").[13] What's more, under my negligence theory, $1,600 was proximately (directly) caused by the shipper's carelessness, meaning this money was recoverable in negligence. I was ready to go.

But wait. What about potential defenses? Might there be something buried in the contact or online that cut our legs out? Remember liability waivers?

I took a look, and it turned out there *was* one. It excused the company from damages related to shipping services other than reimbursement for monies paid. I swallowed hard, then thought even harder. A moment later, I had an idea, which we'll get to in a second.

Armed with the facts and the law, I prepared a letter and mailed it to the store owner via Certified Mail, Return Receipt Requested. A week passed, then another. Nothing. It took me

[13] Figuring my friend received at least some part of his $159 packing-and-shipping charge, I chose not split hairs and instead focused exclusively on the cost of the instrument.

three phone calls to finally reach him. When I did, he told me to pound sand. I told him, "We'll see you in court."

Later that day, I filed my friend's small claims complaint. A few weeks later, we had our hearing date. We'd spend about three hours ahead of time preparing, which included walking through his story, studying the documents, and formulating and fine-tuning the necessary legal arguments.

We arrived thirty minutes early. Parking was a hassle, but it didn't matter because we had planned for that. Once inside the courthouse, we went to the courtroom, but it had been switched. Again, because we were early, that wasn't a problem either.

We entered to watch the judge on the bench. She seemed pretty laid back, which was nice. About two minutes before our hearing time, the courtroom door opened and in walked the defendant. He was wearing jeans and a T-shirt and had nothing with him. We were in suits and had a well-organized and tabbed binder that contained exhibits and our argument.

After hearing two other matters, the judge called our case, and we approached the bench. That's where we would make our arguments. Because I represented the plaintiff, I went first. I told the judge my friend's story, as I just described, and offered documents and photos to support it. (The rules for admitting evidence are fairly relaxed in small claims court.)

The defendant went next, jumbling his sentences and points with no documentary proof to support anything he said. His bottom line was that he did everything right. Things happen, so we should blame someone else in the logistics chain, just not him.

But as uncompelling as this factual argument was, he then made a legal one. He reached into his pocket and pulled out the contract. He *did* have a document after all. Highlighted for the judge was the language excusing his company from damages related to shipping services other than reimbursement for monies paid. At the bottom were his signature and my friend's.

He handed the contract to the judge, who studied it, nodding as she read. When she finished, she set down the document and looked at me. "Counsel," she said, "do you have any questions of the defendant?" She folded her arms, leaned back, and waited.

I stood up straight and tugged on my lapels. "I do, Your Honor," I said, reaching for the contract. The judge handed it to me, and I turned to face the defendant.

"You've produced a copy of the contract between yourself and my client, is that right?"

"It is," the defendant said confidently.

"And at paragraph 27, it explains, 'the company is excused from damages related to shipping services other than reimbursement for monies paid.' Do you see that?"

"I do." His smug look began to creep into a smile.

I cocked my head and gazed thoughtfully past his shoulder. I wanted him to know the wheels were turning. I continued. "But your store doesn't perform shipping services, does it?"

He looked like he'd just seen a ghost. He cleared his throat before answering. "I'm sorry?"

"You send parcels *out* for shipping, don't you? I mean, you don't run trucks, conveyors, or planes, do you?"

"Um, no, we don't."

"And you don't employ drivers or pilots, do you?"

"No."

"But you *do* package parcels for *others* to ship, don't you?"

"Yes, that's something we do."

"Actually, that's *all* you do, isn't it?"

He shifted his stance, then mumbled, "Yes, that's all we do."

"So if you don't *ship* parcels and only package them, no service you performed for my client involved or in any way related to 'shipping services,' did it?" I used air quotes for dramatic effect.

"I guess not."

There was the answer I wanted. I knew I could do better.

"It's not 'I *guess* not.' It's *absolutely* not. Isn't that right?"

"Yes."

"And because you didn't perform shipping services for my client, his damages aren't limited to actual monies paid, are they?"

"I guess not."

I prepared to attack his answer. I could tell he knew what was coming.

"I mean, absolutely not," he volunteered.

I smiled to myself, because it's bad form to gloat in court. I returned the contract to the judge. "No further questions, Your Honor."

The judge, her attitude having visibly shifted, looked at the defendant. "Do you have any questions of the plaintiff." He didn't.

The judge concluded our hearing by saying she'd issue a written ruling in the next couple of weeks.

We left court feeling good but not *too* good. As well as it went, there was no sense jinxing things.

True to the judge's word, in two weeks, I received a letter from the court. It was an order awarding my client his full $1,600. I didn't want to call the defendant to demand payment. That would have been bad form. Besides, I knew he'd received the ruling too. If a check didn't come in a few days, I'd call him then.

About a week later, a check for $1,600 arrived from the defendant, made payable to my friend. That night, I met my friend for dinner where I presented him with the check. After we finished eating, I presented him with *that* check too.

So that was my personal experience in small claims court. Take from it the lessons you will. My result was a good one. Whether yours will be, too, I can't know. But I do know that if you pay mind to *my* experiences, you'll give yourself the best shot at winning.

Chapter 21
What's involved in making it a class action?

Small claims are at one end of the legal spectrum; class actions are at the other. Most of the situations I've discussed lend themselves to class-action lawsuits—you know, the ones that are large because they stand to benefit a lot of people.

Before I describe what a class action is, allow me to describe what a class action *isn't.* Though a class action involves a lot of victims (called *absent class members*), not all mass problems qualify as class actions.

For instance, I'm routinely asked to file a class-action lawsuit against the cable company. Why? Because the cable guy didn't show up between 10:00 a.m. and 2:00 p.m. as promised. I'm also invited to sue the news channels. Why? Because the weatherperson always gets it wrong.

A big *no* to both ideas, which I, of course, listen to with respect. So if that's what a class action isn't, what *is* a class action?

A class action is a legal proceeding where one or more plaintiffs bring a lawsuit on behalf of a larger group, known as the class, against one or more defendants for the violation of a civil (as opposed to criminal) law in a way that affects all class members uniformly. Put more simply, where the plaintiff (called the class representative) can prove their case in a way that proves the absent class members' cases, the plaintiff has a certifiable class action.

Now, I say "certifiable" class action for a reason. When the class representative files their lawsuit, it's not technically a class action yet; it's a *putative* class action. This means the lawsuit is an individual case (lacking much leverage) until the plaintiff demonstrates to the judge that the facts, as channeled through the law, satisfy carefully crafted requirements set forth in the court's rules, whether Federal Rule of Civil Procedure 23 or the state counterpart rules.

I won't dig into the technical requirements necessary for a court to certify a putative class action as a class action (I spend an entire semester doing that in my law school class!); I'll just emphasize that common questions (and answers to these questions) must predominate over individualized questions among the absent class members for sufficient cohesiveness to exist to support class certification. Put another way, the same factual or legal questions (and answers to them) need to apply to the entire class.

Class certification is critical because it transforms the class representative's modest individual claim into a sizable (sometimes massive) claim on behalf of perhaps millions of people. Talk about a game-changer! Indeed, following class certification (especially if affirmed following the automatic appeal that

Federal Rule 23 provides), many cases settle because the risk to the defendant is simply too great.

Class actions are important for several reasons. First, they often involve small damages per person, and no lawyer can afford to take a $10, $50, or $100 claim. (Remember Justice Breyer's remark about lunatics and fanatics?) But when combined into a lawsuit on behalf of lots of people, a class action can make a real difference in terms of fairness and market efficiency. (Remember my flat-panel screens case?)

Second, when class-action recoveries are too small to distribute to class members efficiently, the lawyers can often direct the money to a charity. It's a distribution practice known as *cy pres*. The term derives from trust law and is Norman French (not Latin, for a change) for "as near as possible." We invoke this process when the logistics don't permit us to get damages to class members, yet we don't want to return the money recovered to the wrongdoer.

Third, class actions keep people safe. Without them, companies would cut corners and produce shoddy products, including defective airbags, bad drugs, or faulty medical devices. They would also manipulate our financial markets and commit securities fraud.

Class-action lawyers are often described as private attorneys general whose job is to complement the Department of Justice, Federal Trade Commission, and state attorneys general—all of whom are understaffed—to root out wrongdoing and vindicate consumers' rights. Class actions are so essential to a well-functioning society that several other countries have begun adopting our class-action model. We should be grateful that, in our country, a mature class-action process exists that protects us by keeping prices down and products safe.

Of course, I know what you're thinking. Indeed, I think it too. Look at all those attorneys' fees. But here are a few considerations to keep in mind. First, these fees often come years and years after the attorneys file the case. (The flat-panel case took almost a decade from filing to payday.)

Second, during all this time, not only are the lawyers foregoing other revenue-generating opportunities, but they're also often spending millions and millions of their own money to fund the case—a case where the defense lawyers needn't worry about paying expenses because their client is doing it for them.

Third (and related to the previous point), the lawyers aren't getting paid a penny this entire time. Whereas the defense lawyers are getting paid by the hour, the plaintiffs' lawyers have a contingency fee arrangement, meaning if the case loses, they get nothing for their sometimes decades of work.

Fourth, often, lots of law firms participate in a class action. It's not as if all the attorneys' fees go to one person. Instead, they're shared by several firms. (Flat-panel displays involved over one hundred law firms.)

Fifth, once the firms receive their share of the attorneys' fees, they, too, need to distribute them internally, often needing to pay down lines of credit that have mounted during the time the firms went unpaid.

Finally, unlike in a personal injury case, where the lawyers and client agree to a roughly one-third attorneys' fee, in a class action, the judge decides how much the plaintiffs' lawyers will be paid. Sometimes, the approved fee exceeds the time the plaintiffs' lawyers spent on the case; sometimes it's less.

Now that you know what goes into risking it all for the sake of doing good by helping others (a risk and stakes that defense lawyers will never know), I hope you won't look at attorneys' fees and wince as you once did.

The Supreme Court has emphasized the importance of class actions. They enable groups of people to vindicate their rights when each person's claim is too small to justify its own lawsuit. Class actions combine small claims into a larger claim that lawyers are incentivized to prosecute in exchange for the possibility of receiving attorneys' fees for their hard and risky work. This alignment of interests between clients and counsel provides compensation to injured parties, encourages the enforcement of legal rights against defendants who would otherwise skirt liability, and deters corporate wrongdoing.

For all these reasons, class actions—so long as they're responsibly pursued—are important to all of us.

Chapter 22
How legal wellness can make our lives happier

The better you get at fighting back, the easier it becomes. Heck, it becomes second nature. It's like driving a car. Look at all the dangers you know to watch for when you drive. Talk about keeping your head on a swivel!

The same principle holds as it concerns your legal wellness. When you know what to look for as well as what you shouldn't do (because danger lurks around both corners) you'll become proactive and not reactive. And when we avoid schemes, we stay emotionally well, financially well, and legally well. These three tenets of wellness work together, and they're part of an essential system of proactivity that keeps you in good emotional, financial, and legal shape.

Everything I've explained starts with changing your frame of mind. It begins by understanding that you can do something when you're screwed over because you're *not* a victim. Remember, I consider every canceled flight an opportunity to win. And before long, you'll look at adversity this way, too. Simply put, it's essential to take care of yourself because nobody else will. For if you don't have your wits about you and your eyes open, someone will surely take advantage of you.

As I said to start this book, I'm not giving you legal advice. Without an attorney-client relationship with you, I lack the ability to apply my knowledge to your specific situation, which means I can't understand how the law affects your legal rights. For these reasons, I've not told you *what* to do. I've instead provided you with legal information to raise your awareness, so you'll be better able to spot issues and deal with them productively and preventively.

If you work on developing the proactive mindset I've described, when the bottom falls out for everyone else, it won't for you. Because let's face it—you live in a world that's bound to cheat you. But armed with the information and tools I've shared, you now possess the legal awareness you and your family need to stay safe and achieve legal wellness.

Appendix A: Forced Arbitration

In its 2019 report, "The Truth About Forced Arbitration," the American Association for Justice (AAJ) noted that Americans are more likely to be struck by lightning than win a forced arbitration case *See* https://www.justice.org/resources/research/the-truth-about-forced-arbitration (Report) at 6.

This report also made several troubling observations related to forced arbitration:

Claim Eradication

- AAJ estimates that more than 800 million arbitration provisions affect our everyday lives. *Id.* (citing Imre Stephen Szalai, The Prevalence of Consumer Arbitration Agreements by America's Top Companies, UC Davis Law Review, February 2019, https://lawreview.law.ucdavis.edu/online/vol52/52-online-Szalai.pdf).
- The American Arbitration Association (AAA) and Judicial Arbitration and Mediation Services (JAMS), the two leading consumer arbitration services, recorded

only approximately 30,000 consumer arbitrations from 2014 to 2018—an average of just 6,000 per year. *Id.*

- Despite having hundreds of millions of customers subject to forced arbitration agreements, corporations rarely face arbitration claims. For instance, Amazon has approximately 101 million Prime subscribers yet faced only 15 forced arbitrations over 5 years, GM sells approximately 8 million vehicles sold per year but faced only 5 forced arbitrations over 5 years, and Walmart greets 275 million customers a week but faced just 2 forced arbitrations over 5 years. *Id.*

"Wins" for Consumers

- From 2004 to 2018, only 1,909 consumers won a monetary award in arbitration, which equates to less than the number of people struck by lightning each year in the U.S. *Id.* (citing Lightning Strike Probabilities, National Lightning Safety Institute, http://lightning-safety.com/nlsi_pls/probability.html; Jacob D. Jenson, Andrew L. Vincent, Lightning Injuries, StatPearls, February 19, 2019, https://www.ncbi.nlm.nih.gov/books/ NBK441920/).
- Over five years, only 6.3% of cases arbitrated at the AAA or JAMS resulted in consumers winning a monetary award. *Id.*
- Over a five-year span, AT&T used forced arbitration more than any other corporation, likely emboldened by its Supreme Court victory in *Concepcion. Id.*

- Although nearly 1,000 consumers suffered through forced arbitration between 2014 and 2018, claiming more than $440 million in damages, only 17 consumers won a monetary award, collecting just $376,251. *Id.* at 6–7.

Appendix B

SPECIAL VERDICT FORM

Mr. Depp's Claim Against Ms. Heard

This special verdict form includes each of the statements on which John C. Depp, II bases his claim of defamation against Amber Heard. Answer the questions in accordance with the Court's instructions.

1. As to this statement appearing in the online op-ed, entitled "Amber Heard: I spoke up against sexual violence—and faced our culture's wrath. That has to change" in the *Washington Post*'s online edition:

"I spoke up against sexual violence—and faced our culture's wrath. That has to change."

1(a). Do you find that Mr. Depp has proven all the elements of defamation?

ANSWER YES OR NO: Yes

If you answer question 1(a) "NO," please proceed to question 2.

If you answered "YES," please answer YES or NO to the following questions: Has Mr. Depp proven by a greater weight of the evidence that:

The statement was made or published by Ms. Heard? Yes

The statement was about Mr. Depp? Yes

The statement was false? Yes

The statement has a defamatory implication about Mr. Depp? Yes

The defamatory implication was designed and intended by Ms. Heard? Yes

Due to circumstances surrounding the publication of the statement, it conveyed a defamatory implication to someone who saw it other than Mr. Depp? Yes

1(b). If you answered "YES" to each subpart of question 1(a), answer the following question: do you find that Mr. Depp has proven by clear and convincing evidence that Ms. Heard acted with actual malice?

ANSWER YES OR NO: Yes

{3240786-1, 113633-00003-01}

2. As to this statement appearing in the op-ed entitled "*A Transformative Moment For Women*" in the *Washington Post*'s print edition and the online op-ed "Amber Heard: I spoke up against sexual violence—and faced our culture's wrath. That has to change" in the *Washington Post*'s online edition:

> "Then two years ago, I became a public figure representing domestic abuse, and I felt the full force of our culture's wrath for women who speak out."

2(a). Do you find that Mr. Depp has proven all the elements of defamation?

ANSWER YES OR NO: yes
If you answer question 2(a) "NO," please proceed to question 3.

If you answered "YES," please answer YES or NO to the following questions: Has Mr. Depp proven by a greater weight of the evidence that:

The statement was made or published by Ms. Heard? yes

The statement was about Mr. Depp? yes

The statement was false? yes

The statement has a defamatory implication about Mr. Depp? yes

The defamatory implication was designed and intended by Ms. Heard? yes

Due to circumstances surrounding the publication of the statement, it conveyed a defamatory implication to someone who saw it other than Mr. Depp? yes

2(b). If you answered "YES" to each subpart of question 2(a), answer the following question: do you find that Mr. Depp has proven by clear and convincing evidence that Ms. Heard acted with actual malice?

ANSWER YES OR NO: yes

3. As to this statement appearing in the op-ed entitled "*A Transformative Moment For Women*" in the *Washington Post*'s print edition and the online op-ed "Amber Heard: I spoke up against sexual violence—and faced our culture's wrath. That has to change" in the *Washington Post*'s online edition:

"I had the rare vantage point of seeing, in real time, how institutions protect men accused of abuse."

3(a). Do you find that Mr. Depp has proven all the elements of defamation?

ANSWER YES OR NO: Yes
If you answer question 3(a) "NO," please proceed to question 4.

If you answered "YES," please answer YES or NO to the following questions: Has Mr. Depp proven by a greater weight of the evidence that:

The statement was made or published by Ms. Heard? Yes

The statement was about Mr. Depp? Yes

The statement was false? Yes

The statement has a defamatory implication about Mr. Depp? Yes

The defamatory implication was designed and intended by Ms. Heard? Yes

Due to circumstances surrounding the publication of the statement, it conveyed a defamatory implication to someone who saw it other than Mr. Depp? Yes

3(b). If you answered "YES" to each subpart of question 3(a), answer the following question: do you find that Mr. Depp has proven by clear and convincing evidence that Ms. Heard acted with actual malice?

ANSWER YES OR NO: Yes

Complete Questions 4-5 ONLY if you answered YES to all of questions 1, 2, or 3:

4. As against Amber Heard, state the amount of compensatory damages, if any, you believe John C. Depp, II has proven, by a greater weight of the evidence, that he is entitled to recover:

We, the Jury, award compensatory damages in the amount of $ 10 million .

5. As against Amber Heard state the amount of punitive damages, if any, to which you find John C. Depp, II is entitled to recover:

We, the Jury, award punitive damages in the amount of $ 5 million .

June 1st, 2022
DATE

SIGNATURE OF FOREPERSON

PRINTED NAME OF FOREPERSON

SPECIAL VERDICT FORM

Ms. Heard's Claim Against Mr. Depp

This special verdict form includes each of the statements on which Amber Heard bases her claim of defamation against John C. Depp, II. Answer the questions in accordance with the Court's instructions.

1. As to this statement appearing in the April 8, 2020 online edition of *The Daily Mail*:

"Amber Heard and her friends in the media use fake sexual violence allegations as both a sword and shield, depending on their needs. They have selected some of her sexual violence hoax 'facts' as the sword, inflicting them on the public and Mr. Depp."

1(a). Do you find that Ms. Heard has proven all the elements of defamation?

ANSWER YES OR NO: No

If you answer question 1(a) "NO," please proceed to question 2.

If you answered "YES," please answer YES or NO to the following questions: Has Ms. Heard proven by a greater weight of the evidence that:

Mr. Waldman, while acting as an agent for Mr. Depp, made or published the statement? ________

The statement was about Ms. Heard? ________

The statement was seen by someone other than Ms. Heard? ________

The statement was false? ________

1(b). If you answered "YES" to each subpart of question 1(a), answer the following question: do you find that Ms. Heard has proven by clear and convincing evidence that the statement by Mr. Waldman was made with actual malice?

ANSWER YES OR NO: ________

2. As to this statement appearing in the April 27, 2020 online edition of *The Daily Mail*:

"Quite simply this was an ambush, a hoax. They set Mr. Depp up by calling the cops but the first attempt didn't do the trick. The officers came to the penthouses, thoroughly searched and interviewed, and left after seeing no damage to face or property. So Amber and her friends spilled a little wine and roughed the place up, got their stories straight under the direction of a lawyer and publicist, and then placed a second call to 911."

2(a). Do you find that Ms. Heard has proven all the elements of defamation?

ANSWER YES OR NO: Yes
If you answer question 2(a) "NO," please proceed to question 2.

If you answered "YES," please answer YES or NO to the following questions: Has Ms. Heard proven by a greater weight of the evidence that:

Mr. Waldman, while acting as an agent for Mr. Depp, made or published the statement? Yes

The statement was about Ms. Heard? Yes

The statement was seen by someone other than Ms. Heard? Yes

The statement was false? Yes

2(b). If you answered "YES" to each subpart of question 2(a), answer the following question: do you find that Ms. Heard has proven by clear and convincing evidence that the statement by Mr. Waldman was made with actual malice?

ANSWER YES OR NO: Yes

3. [illegible] o this statement appearing in the April 27, 2020 online [illegible] of *The Daily Mail*:

"[W]e have reached the beginning of the end of Ms. Heard's abuse hoax against Johnny Depp."

3(a). Do you find that Ms. Heard has proven all the elements of defamation?

ANSWER YES OR NO: NO

If you answer question 3(a) "NO," please proceed to question 4.

If you answered "YES," please answer YES or NO to the following questions: Has Ms. Heard proven by a greater weight of the evidence that:

Mr. Waldman, while acting as an agent for Mr. Depp, made or published the statement? __________

The statement was about Ms. Heard? __________

The statement was seen by someone other than Ms. Heard? __________

The statement was false? __________

3(b). If you answered "YES" to each subpart of question 3(a), answer the following question: do you find that Ms. Heard has proven by clear and convincing evidence that the statement by Mr. Waldman was made with actual malice?

ANSWER YES OR NO: __________

Complete Questions 4-5 ONLY if you answered YES to all of questions 1, 2, or 3.

4. As against John C. Depp, II, state the amount of compensatory damages, if any, you believe Amber Heard has proven, by a greater weight of the evidence, that she is entitled to recover:

We, the Jury, award compensatory damages in the amount of $ 2 million.

5. As against John C. Depp, II, state the amount of punitive damages, if any, you to which you find Amber Heard is entitled to recover:

We, the Jury, award punitive damages in the amount of $ 0.

June 1st, 2022
DATE

SIGNATURE OF FOREPERSON

PRINTED NAME OF FOREPERSON

About the Author

Danny Karon received his BA from Indiana University Bloomington and his JD from The Ohio State University Moritz College of Law. He manages Karon LLC, a law firm based in Cleveland, Ohio, where he represents individuals in consumer-fraud, antitrust, and securities-fraud class-action lawsuits. He teaches consumer class actions and complex litigation at the University of Michigan Law School and The Ohio State University Moritz College of Law. Previously, he taught complex litigation at Columbia Law School. He has also lectured at other law schools, including Northwestern, Vanderbilt, Notre Dame, Georgia, and Tulane.

For thirteen years, Danny chaired and taught at the American Bar Association (ABA) National Institute on Class Actions (the nation's leading consumer class-action conference). For five years, he wrote a bimonthly column on class actions and civil justice for Law360. He hosts a website and YouTube channel, www.yourlovablelawyer.com, where he strives to bring legal wellness to all, and he is the author of *The Last Class Action*, a legal thriller. Finally, he has published multiple law-review and bar-journal articles on consumer and class-action topics, and he lectures nationally for the ABA and other bar associations.